Promises and Lies

The Greed of a Presidential Hopeful

Nena Buenaventura

Copyright

Disclaimer

This work of fiction is a satirical commentary on political maneuvering, media manipulation, and the dangers of blind faith. While inspired by real-world events, the characters, events, and situations depicted within are entirely fictional and should not be interpreted as factual accounts or representations of any specific individual or political entity.

The novel utilizes humor and exaggeration to explore the themes of deception, corruption, and the fragility of truth in the public sphere. It is presented as a cautionary tale, highlighting the importance of critical thinking, independent verification of information, and holding leaders accountable for their actions.

This disclaimer serves to clarify the following:

* No real-world events or individuals are

directly mirrored within this fictional narrative. Any similarities to real-world occurrences are purely coincidental and unintentional.

* This story is not intended to endorse any specific political ideology or viewpoint. Its purpose is to stimulate critical thought and discussion regarding the complexities of political systems and the impact of individual choices within them.

* The fictionalized events and characters in this novel should not be interpreted as factual representations of any real-world political figures or events.

This story is a work of imagination and should be enjoyed as such. Please engage with the themes and ideas presented within the context of a fictional narrative.

Table of Contents

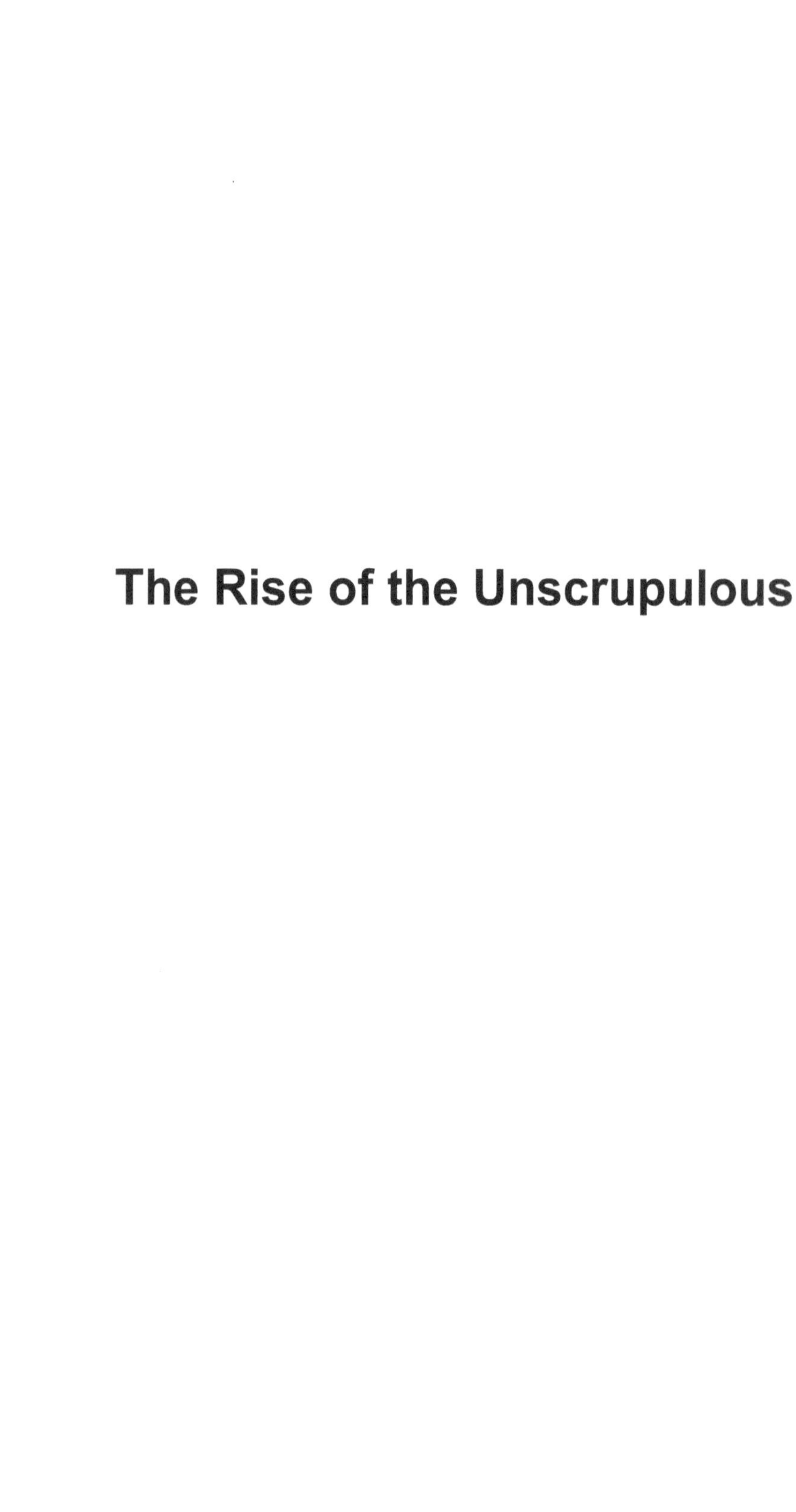

The Rise of the Unscrupulous

Meet Your New Savior

Gerald Grindle stood on the podium, bathed in the spotlight like a lion awaiting his prey. With his charismatic grin plastered across his face, he held the crowd captive, their eyes glimmering with misplaced hope. He was a man draped in the fabric of promises, threading the narrative of struggle and salvation together with the deftness of a seasoned magician pulling rabbits from hats.

"Ladies and gentlemen, I am here to save you!" he boomed, and the crowd erupted into applause, a symphony of clapping hands drowning out any rational thought. With each wave of his hands, he spun tales of prosperity that danced like sugarplums in their minds. Gerald was not merely a politician; he was their personal savior, the beacon of light in their bleak existence.

He promised them the moon, the stars, and a cornucopia of solutions to their dilemmas. "Who needs a plan when you have a promise?" he teased, winking at his audience as they threw caution to the wind. It was a whimsical ride on the carousel of optimism, and they were all too eager to take the leap into the abyss of uncertainty, buoyed by the audacity of his charm.

The swagger with which he dismissed tough questions was akin to a magician sauntering away from an empty sleeve, leaving them bewildered and delighted. Gerald Grindle was indeed a new kind of savior, draped in the luxurious cloak of vague commitments, and the crowd soaked it all in like a sponge starved for water in a desert of reality.

But as the sound of their laughter vibrated through the air, one couldn't help but wonder how long this enchanting facade would last. Beneath the shimmering surface of exuberance lay the undercurrents of doubt, lurking unseen. Would the wave of euphoria crash into the rocky shores of reality, or would they continue to ride the crest of Grindle's delightful promises? The stage was set, and the tension thickened like smoke in a room full of illusionists, leaving one question dangling in the air: what would happen when the curtain finally fell?

The Art of the Pitch

Gerald Grindle was a master of illusion, his charisma dripping like honey on a summer day, sweet and sticky, drawing followers into a web of promises that sparkled but lacked substance. Each word fell from his lips like a magic trick, leaving audiences enchanted yet utterly befuddled. He stood before them, slicked back hair glistening under the bright lights, a grin plastered on his face as he sold them dreams with the finesse of a carnival barker hawking the latest and greatest delights.

Step right up, folks! What if I told you your struggles are only a heart's wish away from being solved? What if your dreams weren't just dreams but the blueprints for your future? It was like stepping into a theater; each line punctuated by gasps and laughter, lights flickering as if in applause for his performance. In this grand spectacle, reality was but a prop, and optimism was the leading star, clouding judgment with its enticing glow.

The air thick with anticipation, the collection of eager faces became a sea of expectation. And yet, it was all reminiscent of an infomercial directed by a comedian high on caffeine—quick cuts to success stories that were as elusive as fairytale endings. With every promise, Grindle launched them into a blissful reverie, blinding them to the hollowness echoing beneath. Each pitch was a balloon, beautifully crafted, drifting into the sky, leaving behind a trail of colorful illusions that vanished the moment they were touched by the bitter hands of reality.

But there lurked an undercurrent of irony, a playful chorus of naysayers disguised as devoted followers, silently chuckling as they rode the wave of fantastical claims. In his wake, the leader left a trail of sticky notes fluttering away in the wind—promises made and broken, visions proclaimed and forgotten. As this chaotic carnival throbbed with lively music, the more astute onlookers found themselves mediated between laughter and disbelief, pinching themselves to ensure they weren't merely stuck in a wildly comedic nightmare.

Yet, as the rhetoric reached a fevered pitch, the tension began to ripple through the crowd—would the next trick reveal the magician's true face, or would it simply be another smoke and mirrors act? As the curtain pulled tighter around this spectacle, the anticipation curled around their throats, a warning whisper of what lay ahead: could their blind faith withstand the inevitable unraveling of the charade?

Promises as Sticky Notes

Gerald Grindle stood before the crowd, his charm radiating like a neon sign in a dark alley. He was a master of theatrics, each word draped in the silk of promise, wrapped loosely like sticky notes fluttering in the wind. "I will fix education! I will lower taxes! I will bring about the dawn of a new era!" The audience erupted in cheers, yet each promise was as ephemeral as the paper it was scribbled on, leaving all assembled hungry for the substance that never quite materialized.

As Grindle dazzled the masses with his grand declarations, the reality of their weight hit like an overripe fruit—a mix of optimism and impending disappointment. His promises flitted around the room, sticking momentarily to the hearts of voters before sliding off into a sea of uncertainty. "We'll have better healthcare! A jobs program so good you won't believe it!" he exclaimed, each statement dancing on the precipice of credibility yet never quite taking the leap. The sticky notes of his assurances lay scattered on the ground behind him, blown away by the winds of reality.

Yet, despite the transient nature of his declarations, the audience remained enamored, their faith stuck like glue to those elusive notes. They laughed, they cheered, but deep down echoed a gnawing feeling of something amiss—like a surreal comedy where the punchline was constantly out of reach. In the fog of enthusiasm, it was easy to forget that sticky notes could be peeled away, discarded without a second thought, a gaping reminder that Grindle's promises held the same potential to vanish at the first sign of scrutiny. And therein lay the tension; could they cling to hope or were they destined to witness the grand unraveling of their cherished illusions?

A Historical Perspective on Hot Air

The Grandeur of Previous Blunders

As Gerald Grindle stood on the grand stage, his voice booming through the speakers, one could not help but recall the historical blunders of leaders who echoed similar empty rhetoric. It was as if the past had come alive, parading before the zealous crowd that cheered every vacuous promise. History had shown time and again how the sweet allure of false promises could seduce even the most rational minds into a stupor of adoration for their would-be saviors.

With each exaggerated claim about prosperity and grandeur, the echoes of prior leaders resonated, reminders of misguided trust and unfulfilled dreams. Citizens who had once held their heads high, burdened by the weight of broken promises, seemed to sway hypnotically in unison, as Grindle spun his web of charm and illusion. The past was not just a distant memory; it was a vivid cautionary tale alive in the laughter of the crowd, oblivious to the irony of their adoration.

Yet, as the crowd cheered louder, one could almost hear the whispers of historical blunders shaking their heads in despair, haunting reminders of the folly that comes with blind loyalty. The air crackled with the tension of a foreboding repeat, as the stage set for another inevitable farce loomed larger, shadows of previous leaders swirling ominously beneath the bright lights. In that moment, something shifted; a smirk exchanged among onlookers hinted that the humor of it all was not lost, even amidst the grandeur of gullibility.

Lessons Ignored

As the electorate clamored for change, they often glanced at the annals of history, yet none dared to delve deeply enough to grasp the seismic echoes of their past. Gerald Grindle emerged like a magician from the shadows, with the audacity to perform tricks so transparent that even the most gullible spectators could see the strings. But witnessing the grand performance was one thing; comprehending the messy truths behind it was another entirely. Those who had been so engrossed never seemed to recall the burnt ends of previous leaders' reigns, nor the chaos left in their wake.

Time and again, in vivid colors and exaggerated strokes, history painted the follies of leaders who, much like Grindle, charmed the masses with promises that danced on the tip of their tongues like butterflies. Yet, the very voters who had once stood disillusioned forgotten tragedies now enthusiastically lined up, ready to be dazzled once more, equipped with the same empty expectations. The irony was thick enough to slice; it danced in the air with a mocking laugh, as though the spirits of past leaders were whispering warnings that were immediately drowned out by Grindle's ever-increasing crescendo of uproarious soundbites.

But alas, the allure of a shiny puppet show was too intoxicating, and the whispers drowned beneath the thunderous applause of the crowd. In this comical farce, the golden window promised to fling open to prosperity instead remained stubbornly shut, locked tight with the keys of denial. Tears of laughter mingled with those of despair as citizens veered blindly towards the comedic oblivion of their own making, dysfunctionally blissful in their ignorance—a cacophony of lessons ignored, ever echoing the absurd reality they had chosen to embrace.

Rhetoric and Reality: A Comedy of Errors

As Gerald Grindle's grandiloquent speeches echoed through the fervent crowds, one could pause to marvel at the magnitude of his promises—replete with glittering visions that sparkled brighter than confetti at a New Year's Eve bash. Yet, as history would have it, such lofty rhetoric rarely materializes; in fact, history presents a litany of leaders who spun similar webs of empty words, leaving behind a legacy marked by hilariously catastrophic failures. Grindle was simply the latest in a long line of individuals who mistook bluster for substance.

The very essence of his campaign unfolded like a Shakespearean comedy, rife with mistaken identities and comedic timing. While he promised to lift the nation from its trials and tribulations, the reality stood in stark contrast—remnants of prior leaders—a veritable graveyard of promises unkept, littered with the disillusioned remains of those who once eagerly believed. However, the voters, like a group of bemused spectators at a badly staged play, seemed ready to overlook the looming shadows of stupidity and blind optimism, perhaps wishing for a different ending this time around.

Yet, with each rally came the unmistakable whiff of absurdity—a spectacle akin to a circus with Grindle as the ringmaster, captivating the audience with dazzling tricks that were more illusion than reality. His rhetoric sparkled, and the crowds ate it up, ever more convinced that beneath the layers of hot air lay tangible solutions to their problems. If only they had heeded the tales of their predecessors, but alas! The laughter around the clownish display seems to have drowned their critical thinking in a pool of cheerful delusion.

The Campaign Begins

Step Right Up to the Show!

Th e air was electric, crackling like a live wire as Gerald Grindle stood center stage, a master showman ready to dazzle the adoring crowd. Step right up, folks! he boomed, his voice echoing through the makeshift arena of folding chairs and colorful banners. You won't want to miss this! A spectacle of promises like you've never seen before!

With the click of a button, a flurry of confetti erupted above him, showering the audience in a kaleidoscope of colors. It was a performance worthy of Broadway, yet behind the curtain, reality lay glaringly naked. Grindle's promises swirled around them like cotton candy, sweet and airy, yet they tasted of nothing at all. Health care for all! Jobs galore! Unicorns! he exclaimed, his proclamation punctuated by a grandiose wave of his arm, eliciting cheers that echoed off the walls like fireworks. A rapturous spell had been cast, and logic, like a frightened rabbit, stood still and small at the edge of the rabbit hole.

As the crowd's enthusiasm swelled, Grindle began to spin his web of deception, ensnaring the hearts and minds of the audience. Each utterance was a sugar-coated pill, designed to go down smooth, while the bitter aftertaste was conveniently ignored. Let us be the change we want to see! Together, we can accomplish the impossible! The rapture was palpable, but beneath the surface of applause, uncertainty lurked like a lurking beast, waiting for a moment to pounce.

Meanwhile, his top aides, disguised as acrobats, flew around, distributing shiny pamphlets filled with slogans and cheesy graphics. A gleeful, slightly dazed woman in the front row waved her pamphlet like a flag of allegiance, declaring, I'll believe anything for a brighter tomorrow! The absurdity was met with laughter, yet laughter masked a growing unease as the logic of their decisions began to unravel in the glow of the spotlight. After all, would tomorrow ever come if they were too busy reveling in today's spectacle?

As Grindle strutted and preened, dazzling the crowds with theatrics, the line between truth and illusion blurred beyond recognition. Who needs policies when we have passion? he roared, sending waves of applause crashing through the crowd. Yet the shadows around the stage seemed to grow longer and darker, mirroring the gathering skepticism lurking among the attendees. Questions buzzed like flies around their ears: How long could the circus continue? How long before the audience woke from this stupor?

The tension mounted as the show rolled on, with Grindle now juggling promises that he had no intention of keeping. I will eradicate poverty! he proclaimed, tossing his arms into the air as if burdened with invisible weights. And there will be gardens of prosperity blooming on every corner! As he made his colorful claims, the whispers began to simmer, doubts creeping like shadows in the back of even the most starry-eyed supporters. Was this all just a dazzling distraction, a mirage in a world that longed for tangible solutions?

As the night drew on and the spectacle reached its zenith, whispers morphed into murmurs and then erupted into rumbles of unease. How long could they ignore the realities of their lives while dancing to Grindle's tune? Laughter erupted as he cracked a joke, but the laughter echoed back, hollow now, as trepidation seeped into the fabric of the gathering. The audience began to sense that they were not mere spectators but unwilling participants in a performance that was destined to culminate in chaos.

Circus Acts: Rallies and Speeches

The air crackled with excitement as the crowd gathered, a motley assembly of colorful signs and enthusiastic cheers, each one more vibrant than the last. Gerald Grindle's campaign launch resembled not just a rally but a dazzling circus, where twinkling lights and loud music masked the hollow promises he skillfully peddled. From the outset, it was clear that this was less about politics and more about performance; the crowd's exuberance seemed choreographed, synchronized with the rhythm of Grindle's grandiloquent proclamations.

With every speech he delivered, Grindle sat atop his metaphorical unicycle, balancing on the thin line between absurdity and charisma. He wooed his audience like a ringmaster wielding a whip of words, each crack reverberating with exaggerated assertions that whisked them away from reason. Rallies became a flamboyant spectacle, a theatrical display filled with overzealous followers who wore their blind adoration like glittering costumes, dazzlingly oblivious to the underlying emptiness of their hero's promises.

Between bursts of laughter and gasps of disbelief, the audience cheered for gimmicks that sparkled more than any policy discussion could. Who needed substance when Grindle was serving up a feast of flashy distractions? Like children at a carnival, they gravitated towards the shiny baubles of his campaign, obliviously swallowing the hollow rhetoric with eager smiles. And yet, in the back of the arena, whispers began to swirl— hints of doubt, an undercurrent of discontent that threatened to erupt just as dramatically as the spectacle in front of them.

Vote for Gimmicks, Not Policies

The air was thick with excitement and streamers, the kind of atmosphere that crackled with anticipation as Gerald Grindle took the stage, a man molded by charisma and equipped with an arsenal of gimmicks. His campaign was less about pixels of policy nerds reaching out to the masses and more about a foot-tapping, star-studded variety show that would make any Saturday night program seem bland by comparison.

As he leaned into the microphone, the crowd erupted, not in discernable political discourse but in an exuberant wave of anticipation for whatever shiny object he was about to unveil. "Why talk about poverty when I can juggle flaming torches and promise unicorns?" Grindle quipped, as if to justify the absence of any substantive negotiation for change. The spectators laughed, clapped, and cheered—not for a new healthcare policy or educational reform, but for the sheer thrill of spectacle.

Before long, it was clear: this was not merely a campaign; it was a circus. And in this circus, the voters had become entranced by the bright colors and theatricality, their cravings for deeper dialogues drowned out by the steady drumbeat of gimmicks that spiraled higher than any vault of policy could ever reach. How had it come to this? Distracted by the shiny baubles that fell from Grindle's lips, the populace soon forgot the very reason they had gathered: to demand real answers.

As Grindle continued, his promises morphed into dazzling illusions, dancing whimsically beyond the grasp of rational thought. "We'll have building-free weekends! Exercise no longer required!" he proclaimed with grandiose flair, and laughter erupted like fireworks, echoing in the hearts of those desperate to believe that at last, someone would liberate them from the shackles of responsible governance.

And therein lay the magnificent absurdity — for while promises of soaring joy spiraled upward, the ground beneath them quaked with the reality of neglected policies and shattered hopes covered in the glitter of half-truths. But who cared? The audience was entranced, already selecting their party hats for a joyous ride down the merry-go-round of his promises, hopeful and unknowing of the storm brewing just beyond the funhouse mirrors of his rhetoric.

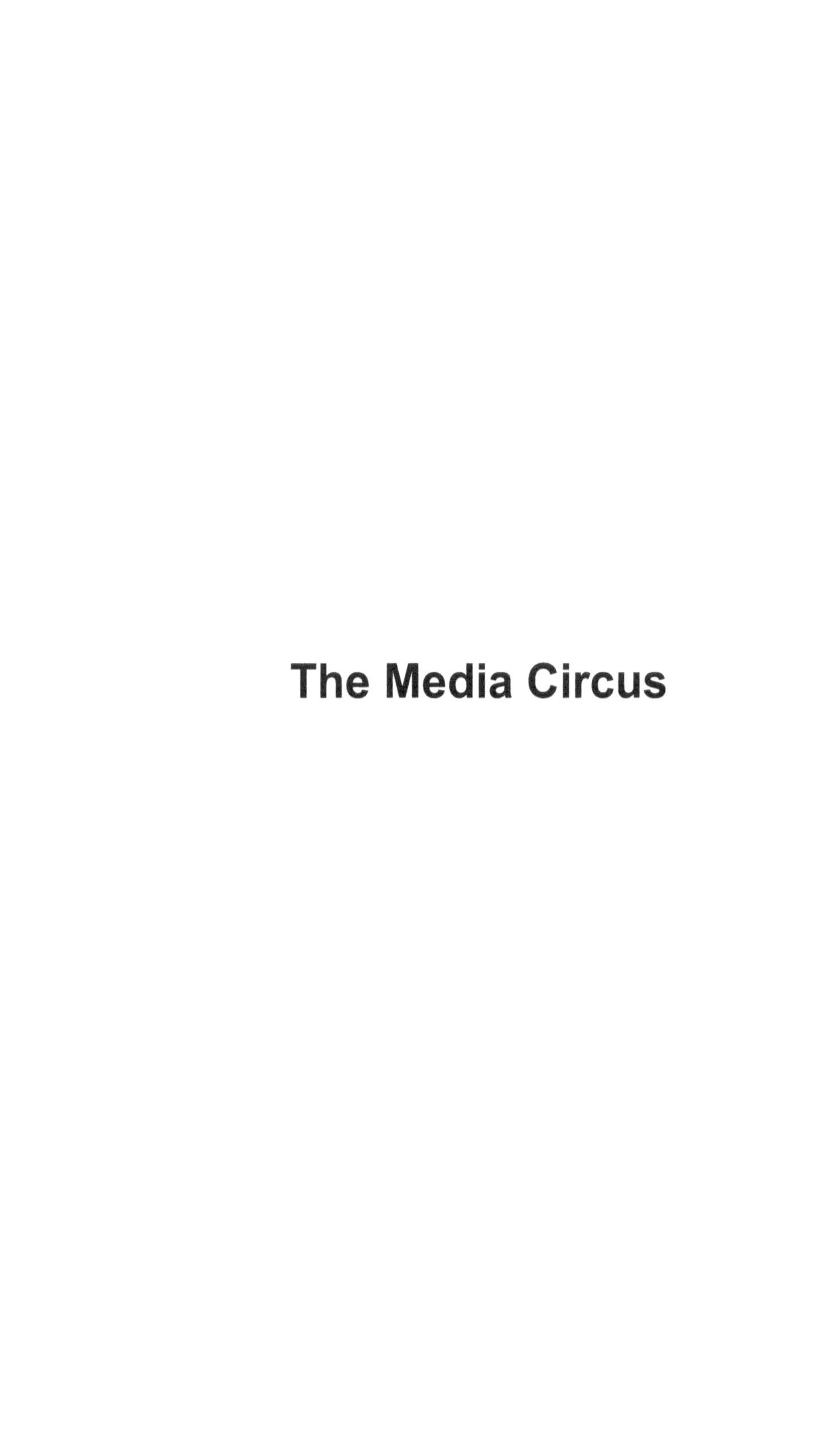

The Media Circus

The Great Debate: Who Wore It Best?

As the lights dimmed and the crowd roared, the great debate approached with all the elegance of a misguided fashion show. Gone were the days of earnest discourse; this cacophony had morphed into a carnival where outfits took precedence over opinions. Gerald Grindle, clad in a suit that shimmered brighter than a disco ball, strutted onto the stage, undoubtedly planning to dazzle the viewers more with his wardrobe than his words.

His opponent, a formidable candidate draped in a power suit that screamed authority, took a deep breath, clearly aware of the uphill battle that lay ahead. The topic of conversation? The future of the nation, but like a designer handbag, it was quickly overshadowed by the question of who was best dressed. The audience—a mix of fashion enthusiasts and political junkies—began to clap and cheer for the bluster of aesthetics rather than the substance of ideas. "Did you see the cut on that suit?" one remarked, while another pondered if they should have brought a notepad to draft postelection fashion reports rather than policy suggestions.

Sound bites flitted through the air like confetti. Each candidate tried to out-quip the other, but the true winners were the stylists behind them. A well-timed wink, a strategic pause, and the audience erupted in cheers as the candidates cajoled and complimented each other's ensembles. Grindle, ever the showman, used the distraction to slip in a promise or two—vague enough to avoid commitment but catchy enough to resonate amidst the applause. It was less about changing the world and more about who had the trendiest retort. "Policies? I'll leave those to my fashion advisor!" he quipped, eliciting laughter that only thickened the atmosphere with absurdity.

And there they stood, two contenders with visions for the nation's future, reduced to mere mannequins on a political runway. The crowd, unperturbed by the growing tension, continued to cheer the candidates and their ridiculous repartee. Sparkling laughter echoed through the auditorium, while the real issues weighed heavy, smothered under layers of fabric and farce. It became clear that this debate had morphed from a battle of ideas into a theatrical display that signaled the rise of a disturbing trend—policy had become secondary to performance. With each passing moment, their values donned a mask, buried somewhere beneath the glitzy veneer.

But would they notice when the lights dimmed for good? Or would they remain oblivious to their own volition, fully engrossed in the spectacle? As the debate reached its climax, and the candidates prepared for their final pitches, the air crackled with anticipation and a touch of dread. The audience's laughter rang hollow, a comedic overture for what was to come.

Sound bites Over Substance

As the campaign train rolled on, the electorate squinted through a haze of glittering promises, often losing sight of the actual issues at hand. Grindle, with his charisma dialed up to eleven, masterfully played the media like a seasoned juggler, tossing sound bites into the air while the substance slipped quietly under the rug. It was a great show, and everyone was eager for their next fix of affable nonsense, pitched by a man who could charm the pants off a statute.

At the debates, where one might assume serious dialogue would reign, the theater reached near delirium. Each candidate strutted like peacocks, but Grindle, ever the dramatist, knew the crowd craved pizzazz. When he declared, If you want to see growth, just look at the flourishing flowers in my garden! it drew laughter and raucous applause. The audience lapped it up, forgetting that they hadn't learned a single policy point in the exchange. This was the dance of distraction, a crafty preparation of fluff that drowned out any kernel of truth.

Meanwhile, the real issues—job losses, healthcare, or the environmental crisis—were consigned to the shadows, labeled as 'too boring' for the main act. Audiences watched, entranced by the spectacle, blissfully unaware as the heart of their concerns was treated like yesterday's trash. With every witticism Grindle threw, real problems swirled farther into oblivion, lost among the confetti of catchy phrases that lit up the moment but promised nothing for the future.

As the months rolled on, dissension began to bubble beneath the surface. Critics tried to highlight the absurdity, with commentators weeping over the state of political discourse. But their voices were drowned out by the chorus of fans clamoring for another round of Grindle's charisma, illustrating the divide between the vast superficiality that captivated the masses and the lurking, unnerving truth that shadows were silently inching closer.

All eyes turned to the sky as Grindle prepared to unveil his grand finale at the rally—his most outrageous sound bite yet. As the crowd buzzed with excitement, there was a palpable tension in the air, like a balloon stretched too tight. Would this sparkling moment obliterate the desert of content that came before? All that remained was the hope that when the laughter faded, the electorate would finally wake to realize that beneath the gleaming surface lay a void where substance was meant to flourish.

Spin Doctors: The Real Wizards

As the spotlight blazed on Gerald Grindle, a team of meticulously groomed spin doctors flitted around like elegant magicians, conjuring a fabrication of reality that dazzled the senses. They could obscure the truth with a mere wave of their hands, cultivating an image of competence and care so captivating that the citizens were left believing their own illusions. Each carefully crafted statement draped in positivity shimmered like gold, while the harsh reality became a distant memory, fading into the background.

These tactful wizards artfully spun narrative after narrative, weaving a tapestry of promises adorned with glitzy fabrications meant to beguile the most discerning audience. "It's all about the optics," they whispered, their voices laden with the urgency of a slick sales pitch. With just the right mix of charisma and polished rhetoric, Grindle's supporters were transformed into ardent believers, eagerly clapping along to the show, convinced that the road ahead was paved in gold.

Yet, beneath the surface of glamour and charm, a parched desert of disillusion lay waiting. The spin doctors didn't merely reshape reality; they had built a precarious stage upon smoke and mirrors, poised delicately on the edge of a cliff. As Grindle's reputation soared, some began to detect the tremors of absurdity lurking beneath the applause. But any dissent was greeted with a grand flourish—a chorus of support that drowned out the panicked whispers of doubt. Could the spell, so masterfully woven, be undone by mere mortals?

As the election approached, the tension thickened, like the air before a storm. The wizards worked overtime, crafting responses to inevitable scandals and pitfalls with relentless zeal. Confidence surged among Grindle's camp, yet behind closed doors, uncertainty simmered. Could they maintain the illusion, or would a crumbling facade reveal the caricature beneath? Time would tell, but it wouldn't be long before the punchline to this farce had everyone buckling in for a hysterical revelation, leaving them to question whether they had been nothing more than willing participants in a jest played on them by their own blind trust.

The Promises of a Lifetime

The Grand Vision Board

Gerald Grindle's vision board was a spectacle reminiscent of a child's art project gone wildly out of control. Affixed with glitter and stickers, it showcased his "promises" as colorful illustrations that lacked any real substance. The board resembled a mix between a fairytale and a circus, with images of flying cars, unicorns providing healthcare, and an unlimited supply of ice cream for all. Here, in this whimsical display, Grindle portrayed himself not just as a politician but as the fairy godfather of his constituents' dreams, complete with sparkles of optimism that made the absurd seem attainable.

Those who gathered around the board couldn't help but chuckle nervously; the promises were ludicrous, each more impractical than the last. "Imagine a world where students graduate debt-free!" one bright pink sticky note proclaimed, floating just above a drawing of a piggy bank bursting with cash. Beneath it, another spelled out, "Free vacations for every citizen!" The crowd laughed, unsure if they were supposed to take Grindle's agenda seriously or not. Confusion hung in the air like the smell of burnt popcorn at a carnival, making it both amusing and unsettling.

Grindle himself stood nearby, beaming with pride as people snapped selfies with his masterpiece. "This, my friends, is just a taste of what we can accomplish together!" he declared, his arms outstretched as if he were about to pull a rabbit out of a hat. But with every promise written on that board, the reality of governance seemed to slip further into the realm of fairy tales. Those present, entranced by the spectacle, found themselves caught in the web of his charm, unaware that their hopes were being pinned to a creation as flimsy as the sticky notes that adorned it.

Promises Made in Ink and Blood

As Gerald Grindle stood before the captive audience at the largest rally of his campaign, he unfurled yet another vision that shimmered like silver but felt as substantial as soap bubbles. Parked behind him was his infamous vision board, a colorful collage of promises fashioned from the vibrant scraps of imagination and hope. It glittered in the sunlight, a kaleidoscope of what could be but was ever unfurling with an impracticality that could make even a jester cringe.

Imagine! he bellowed, waving his arms dramatically, A society where every child is guaranteed a plushie unicorn alongside their education! A promise to uplift spirits and grades alike! The crowd erupted into applause, cheers mixed with laughter, but the air felt dense—a palpable tension brewing, as if the collective joy was a tonic masking deeper worries.

Yet, poised on the edge of blissful ignorance, the audience didn't catch the slipknot in Grindle's rhetoric. Promises made in ink and blood, both romantic and treacherous, floated like whispers among the voters. They yearned for change, for meaning, but willingly accepted the enchanted script he wrote in juicy red ink while ignoring the frayed edges of truth. The fleeting notes stuck to the walls of their minds, slowly unraveling but still decorated with glimmers of false hope.

Time ticked away, and as he moved to his next fanciful pledge—a tax rebate delivered via ice cream truck—an audible, collective gasp coursed through the crowd. There it was: a question rising from the back, a voice slicing through the laughter with a clarity that cut deeper than a sword. "But how, Gerald? How will you afford these fantastical delights?" The laughter faltered, and tension weaved itself into the fabric of the moment, awareness creeping through previously unquestioning minds.

Below the sweetness of Grindle's sugary promises lay a darker reality, one made of inky shadows and blood-red implications. The truth—another fleeting character in this political theatre—lurched forward, ready to undermine the farcical display. Silent minds awakened, darting eyes seeking the whispers of reality concealed beneath Grindle's grandiose schemes. The question lingered in the air, a spark flickering against the backdrop of painted dreams, setting the stage for a reckoning both humorous and horrifying.

As Grindle waved goodbye, the crowd burst into a round of cheers, but laughter now masked uncertainty, nearly tangible in its weight. The tension sweetened like the icing on a beautifully baked lie, tempting yet suspicious, drawing them into the delicious chaos of his rhetoric. Would anyone dare to peel back the layers of his sugary promises? Or would they remain stuck in the candy-coated web of his charming facade?

Unveiling the Magic Wand

Gerald Grindle had a flair for the dramatic, and his latest prop was nothing short of spectacular—a whimsical magic wand that would make even the greatest illusionists green with envy. Crafted from an exotic blend of sparkly tape and cardboard, this wand was a beacon of hope, or at least that's what Grindle wanted his adoring followers to believe. With each wave of his hand, he promised to transform their desperate realities into glittering utopias, where jobs magically appeared, the economy flourished, and every household received a free unicorn. Who could resist such a spectacle?

The audience, captivated by the shiny allure, clapped fervently. It was a scene reminiscent of kids at a carnival, entranced by the colorful balloons and giant stuffed animals. But as Grindle continued his performance, a few cautious voices emerged from the crowd. "But Gerald, can you really fix our broken roads just by waving that thing around?" they questioned, their skepticism barely masked beneath layers of hope.

Yet, the charm of the wand was undeniable. It became a symbol of all the fanciful promises Grindle made, each one stickier than the last—like a note left too long on a fridge door. He waved it fiercely, demanding people to imagine a world where their troubles could be whisked away. Those who dared to entertain these notions found themselves torn. Could they dismiss the enchanter's tricks, or should they dive headfirst into this captivating sea of absurd possibilities?

With magic in the air and whispers of revolution echoing in the background, the tension began to build. A showdown loomed on the horizon—where the allure of Grindle's wand would meet the hard realities of the world outside. The magic, as charming as it appeared, was about to face its greatest test: the inevitable question of how long the spell could last before it unraveled into thin air.

A Misguided Loyalty

The Followers: Heroes or Henchmen?

Grindle's followers play both hero and henchman, defending delusions with absurd fervor. In the vibrant rallying cries of "Change is here!" and "You can't spell 'Grindle' without 'Win'," they transformed into an army of enthusiasts, marching under the banner of fantasy, oblivious to the reality dancing just outside their gilded bubbles. Like valiant knights of yore, they donned their armor made of catchy slogans and catchy hashtags, wielding smartphones like swords, ready to joust against any dissent like medieval jesters defending their king.

Blind faith in Grindle leads followers to financial despair, but they carry on unabated. As bills piled up and bank accounts dwindled to echoes of their former selves, they brushed it off, murmuring "The economy is just in a transition phase!" with all the conviction of a telemarketer selling a time-share in Atlantis. Fervently waving their foam fingers, they clung to their belief that tomorrow would dawn brighter, that one more invigorating rally would surely extend the lifeline of their dreams, even as their delusions crumbled like soggy popcorn at a bad movie.

Grindle's followers form a choir, echoing promises while silencing dissent with enthusiasm. The discordant yet harmonious blend of chants, "We believe in Gerald!" pierced the air like a rallying anthem, drowning out the rustling whispers of skepticism. They transformed skepticism into a forgotten melody, an irritating background noise as they swayed to their own fervent tunes, creating a wall of sound that kept dissenters at bay. But underneath the surface, cracks began to appear in this whimsical facade of devotion, hinting at the deeper conflicts and comedic tension that simmered just beneath the surface, about to erupt into a cacophony of absurdity.

Blind Faith and Handy Pockets

The scene was set; a vibrant rally sprawled across the town square, all glittering signs and raucous cheer. Gerald Grindle stood at the center, his charismatic smile wrapping around the audience like a warm, fuzzy blanket in the dead of winter. The faithful, eyes sparkling with hope-like lemmings at the edge of a cliff, cheered as he spoke of shimmering futures and promises painted in bold strokes of nonsense. If there was one thing they were loyal to, it was the idea that their savior could do no wrong, even as the ground beneath them began to wobble.

Like moths to a flame, they flocked to Grindle, clutching their handy pockets that bulged with the "smart investments" he had swooped in to sell them. The whispers of skepticism floated around them like ghosts, but they were drowned out by the melodious symphony of blind faith. It was a ridiculous ballet where sanity had exchanged places with fervor; where reason had been boxed up and stuffed into the pockets that held nothing but receipts for the dreams that were eluding them. However, as evening shadows crept in, the sunlight began to expose the cracks in their faith.

Meanwhile, the faithful trotted along, keeping a tight grip on their handy pockets, blissfully unaware that those pockets were not just filled with hard-earned cash but also with their ability to think critically. The more they cheered, the more they found their wallets emptying, a delightful paradox that tickled the edges of irony. Each rally only added to the hollow echo of their laughter, a chorus that drowned out their budgetary woes, until that laughter turned into a cacophonous realization that reverberated disturbingly within their minds.

As Grindle launched into his grand finale of promises, those handy pockets began to feel laden with a different kind of weight—one forged from gut-wrenching doubt. Could it be that the sparkly dreams crafted by their charming leader were nothing more than a mirage? The murmur of discontent began to swirl among the crowd, like the clattering of spoons in a tin cup, echoing the hope that it wouldn't end like so many before—covered in a thick layer of financial despair. Yet, loyalty kept them rooted to the ground, unwilling to sever the strings that tied their fate to Grindle.

But alas, shadows grow long, and the flicker of reality was creeping in all around them. It was a perfect storm of witless wonderment, where the handy pockets that once held tangible dreams now seemed to echo with the hollowness of unfulfilled promises. The tension in the air thickened, a palpable sensation that rippled through the gathered masses, waiting for a moment to break, waiting for the punchline of this cruel joke to land.

The Choir of Echoes

In the dimly lit corners of Grindle's rallies, a peculiar phenomenon began to unfold. His followers, once a ragtag assemblage of everyday citizens, morphed into an enthusiastic choir, harmonizing with every promise that spilled from their leader's lips. Each note of hope sounded melodious, a surreal testament to the human ability to suspend disbelief. As they sang praises, they crafted a reality adorned with shimmering illusions where every echo became a verse praising the savior of the people.

Their voices crescendoed in a raucous symphony, drowing out dissent like a well-rehearsed performance, drowning out the less fortunate folk left fumbling for rational discourse. To the choir, the uncertainty of

Grindle's grandiloquent promises took on an irresistible cadence, and the absurd became anthemic. The repetitive refrains of, "Together, we will rise!" and "A better tomorrow is just a song away!" veiled the cracks in their collective consciousness.

And yet, as the exhilaration reached fever pitch, a rift began to form. Dissenters emerged from the shadows, mere whispers at first, questioning the harmonized façade. Their dissonant chords poked holes in the euphoric swell, reminding the followers that the chorus might be nothing more than an echo chamber. The dichotomy of faith and reason began to clash, resonating unevenly as the once indomitable music faltered, leaving a lingering discord that promised a reckoning.

The Game of Lies

Truth vs. Convenient Fabrications

As the spotlight shone brightly on Gerald Grindle, the master of misdirection, his convenient fabrications wove a tapestry of illusion that glimmered more alluringly than any truth. He stood at the podium, an ethereal figure shrouded in the haze of well-scripted drama, beckoning his audience to ignore the nagging doubts that gripped their reason like a vice. To the throng before him, he became the epitome of hope—a distraction from the raw, cold truth of governance that lurked just beyond the curtain of his performance.

In a world where facts were mere suggestions, Grindle's fabrications glided believably off his tongue, tantalizingly persuasive and ever so meticulously crafted. The crowd gasped at promises of a perfect economy, a utopia where everyone thrived, and all troubles melted away like ice cream on a July afternoon. Little did they know that behind the fanfare lay a reality riddled with uncertainty—a truth that spoke of struggles, challenges, and the tedious labor it took to craft a functional society.

As the confetti settled, amidst cheers and laughter, the undercurrents of skepticism began to swirl, threatening to disrupt the euphoric dance orchestrated by Grindle. Whispering doubts crept into conversations, split-second glances exchanged like wary spies as the citizens, intoxicated by his charm, wrestled with the frantic tug-of-war between what they genuinely sought and the intoxicating comfort of what he so conveniently fabricated. It was a growing chasm, and with each laugh that erupted from the crowd, the abyss deepened, shimmering ominously between the reverent and the ridiculous.

The Emergence of Dystopia

As Gerald Grindle's tenure progressed, the once colorful promises of a brighter future began to fray at the edges, revealing the stark gray of a dawning dystopia. While he dazzled crowds with his infomercial flair, the policies that emerged bore little resemblance to the vibrant vision painted during his campaign. It was as if the world had transformed into one of those absurd paintings where the colors dripped into murky puddles, leaving behind ghostly outlines of what could have been.

Citizens, caught in a whirlwind of optimism, were blissfully unaware that the fantastical policies implemented were like candy-coated lies, sweet on the surface but rotting at the core. The air was thick with the smell of desperation masked by laughter; humor became the coping mechanism as ordinary people attempted to navigate through the ruins of Grindle's grand designs. Among the absurdity, a new language emerged—a blend of sarcasm and irony, spoken fluently by those who dared to question just how many unicorns were truly promised.

Yet, as the laughter echoed through the streets, a sense of foreboding began to creep in. The comical fallout of his whimsical mandates took a turn towards the bizarre, illustrating life in Grindle's dystopia. Infrastructure crumbled while citizens painted signs proclaiming "More Rainbows!" in a futile bid for hopeful imagery amidst chaos. Meanwhile, the invisible walls of Grindle's facade began to crack, hinting at the true extent of absurdity lurking beneath. Increasingly, it felt as though the twilight of reason had settled over the land, draping it in the dark but oddly amusing cloak of surrealism.

Witless Wonders: The Audience Reaction

As Gerald Grindle unfurled his tapestry of whimsical lies, audiences found themselves entwined in a surreal spectacle. Crowded auditoriums buzzed with an electrifying mix of laughter and disbelief, as his outlandish claims danced dangerously close to the absurd. With every blinkered promise of prosperity, the attendees shared fleeting glances, half-convinced they had snuck into a bizarre circus rather than a political event.

Grindle, bright as a peacock and twice as loud, promised to transform their humble hamlets into glittering utopias overnight. The crowd roared with laughter—was this theatrical bravado or an earnest plea? He punctuated each ludicrous statement with exaggerated gestures, coaxing peals of laughter from audiences that dared not question whether their sanity was slipping. This was not just a campaign; it was an avant-garde performance arts festival.

But as the laughter evolved into a strange, unsteady rhythm, a creeping tension underlay the merriment. Some audience members were caught in a battle of wits and wills, grappling with the absurdity of Grindle's rhetoric. Was it possible that they were unwitting participants in a grand folly? As they leaned forward, desperate for clarity amidst the chaos, others echoed the ridiculous yet embraced the ignorance like a comforting blanket—after all, the absurd was easier to digest than the bitter truth of governance.

In the midst of this cacophony, the ghost of common sense lurked, whispering sweet nothings that begged for attention while being drowned out by the laughter and applause. Grindle's promises, like a piñata stuffed with confetti and dreams, were fun to smash open. Yet as the integrity of their dreams hung tantalizingly just out of reach, the haunting question loomed: were they all just witless wonders, gleefully sticking their heads in the sand whilst the world crumbled around them?

What began as a light-hearted jest had morphed into a gripping drama where excitement clashed with unshakeable ignorance. The theatrics escalated, creating a tornado of laughter and gnawing doubt, making it all too clear that in this game of lies, the audience was both the punchline and the wise fool, teetering precariously between fun and farce.

When Reality Sets In

The Broken Glass of Hopes

As Grindle's governance unfolded, the scenario morphed into a comedic tragedy—broken glass littering the streets where hopes had once glistened. Citizens ambled through these debris-laden paths, stepping on their shattered dreams, which crunched beneath their feet like crushed expectations.

Every campaign promise that had promised utopia was now a glimmering fragment, reflecting the harsh sunlight onto bewildered faces. Vibrant economy! one shard shouted, while another narrated the tale of Healthcare for everyone! in twisted irony. Hopes that once soared like kites flew only to be ensnared by the reality of Grindle's whimsical policies.

Amidst the debris, an elderly woman named Gertrude knelt, picking up a piece of glass that had once read "End of Economic Woes." She examined it closely, shaking her head with a smirk. She whispered, "Well, that ended up being true, in a way. We have no economy left to worry about." Her neighbors, a group of disillusioned citizens, chuckled dryly as she continued her scavenger hunt for optimism amidst chaos, absurdity their only coping mechanism.

Across the street, a band of hopefuls adorned themselves in makeshift costumes made from the vibrant remnants of campaign flyers, declaring loudly their undying loyalty. "We're here to support our beloved leader!" they bellowed, clutching hollow promises like children clutching teddy bears. Their chants, once infectious, grew tiresome as they stomped through the wreckage of their own unrealized aspirations.

But laughter, that stubborn ember of resilience, flickered in the wreckage. A spontaneous comedy routine erupted among the townsfolk—an absurdity fest where hope had been transformed into hearty laughter. A young man, with an exaggerated performance, gestured at the shattered promises littered about, "Look at all this great potential! Too bad it's reflecting reality instead of prosperity!" His quip ignited a raucous uproar, turning the somber scene into a carnival of jests and jeers.

Yet, as laughter and levity filled the air, the specter of restless discontent loomed, drawing tensions tighter with every chuckle. A palpable shift occurred within the jovial crowd as murmurs of rebellion flickered to life. Their shattered hopes weren't just splintering underfoot—they were igniting flames of realization, turning laughter into a rallying cry for change.

Amidst the merriment, Gertrude rose to her feet, the broken glass reflecting the intensity in her gaze. "If this is the path we're meant to walk, let's reclaim those hopes buried beneath the shards! We may laugh at the absurdity, but let's not forget—we have the strength to reshape our reality from this comedic wreckage!" With her impromptu rallying cry, laughter transformed, no longer a mask for despair, but a catalyst for defiance. The tension bubbled under the surface, a moment ripe for the unexpected.

As the sun dipped lower in the sky, casting elongated shadows over the remnants of hope, the crowd became a haphazard assembly of resolute individuals, each echoing Gertrude's sentiment. It was a strange juxtaposition—a celebration of absurdity and the dawning awareness of their fractured reality, culminating in an electric anticipation for what was to come.

Rescue Mission: Finding Common Sense

In the midst of chaos, a group of well-meaning citizens gathered at the local diner, which had become the de facto headquarters for those attempting to salvage their lost common sense. Each member sat with a cup of steaming coffee and a plethora of half-eaten pastries that conspired against their waistlines, yet they couldn't help but nibble on the absurdity of their current predicament.

Okay, folks, called out Linda, a retired schoolteacher with an impish glint in her eye. We need to map out a rescue mission—Operation Common Sense! Our first target: understanding how we let Grindle's promises puff us up like balloons at a festival!

The group erupted into laughter, but it was tinged with a shared sorrow. Who would have thought their hopes could deflate just as quickly? Each laugh echoed a reality they were trying to face, one absurd promise at a time. "Step one," suggested Tom, a once-ardent supporter of Grindle, now questioning his own judgment. "We make a list of his most outrageous commitments. I'll start: free unicorn rides for everyone!"

With each addition to the list, the diner filled with laughter, but there was an underlying tension—what began as a whimsical gallery of fantastical promises was gradually morphing into a grim realization of how profoundly they had been bamboozled. As they reminisced about how they had cheered wildly, hoping that a sprinkle of Grindle's magic dust would solve all their woes, the weight of their gullibility began to settle in.

As the sun dipped lower in the sky, casting absurd shadows that mirrored the ridiculousness of their plight, the air thickened with determination. "So what's the plan, fearless leader?" asked Marge, her eyes bright but her tone laced with mock seriousness.

Linda leaned in closer, her voice conspiratorial. "We tackle the people who are still under Grindle's spell. We'll share our stories, inject a bit of wisdom into their foggy minds. If this gets messy, we'll have to resort to our secret weapon: humor."

Suddenly, the door swung open, and in walked Bob—the town optimist who unexpectedly read as tragic comic relief. "You all look like you've swapped common sense for this delusion!" he shouted, cheerfully oblivious to the gravity of their mission. The group groaned, but his exuberance was infectious. A glimmer of hope emerged amidst the laughter: perhaps they could turn the tables if they lightened the doom-laden atmosphere with a heavy dose of wit.

Determined, they settled into a rhythm of sardonic camaraderie, concocting absurd scenarios in which Grindle's promises played out hilariously wrong. By the time the diner lights flickered overhead, they were fully armed with jokes, ready to confront their fellow townspeople with laughter as their shield. Yet the uncertainty still loomed. Could humor really pierce through the fog of delusion that held Grindle's followers captive? The answer embraced the delightful absurdity: they had to try.

As the crowd thinned and anxious laughter lingered, the group took one last fortifying gulp of coffee. Bob looked at Linda and said with a grin, "So, do we believe we'll actually make a difference?"

"We might just spark a rocky road to recovery," Linda replied with a wink. With that, the dawn of a hysterically poignant mission to retrieve their common sense had begun, even if it meant braving the absurd together.

The Great Disillusionment

As the dust settled over Grindle's so-called achievements, the once fervent cheers of his supporters transformed into a cacophony of confusion and disbelief. It was a comical sight—a parade of shattered dreams marching down the streets, where confetti made of broken promises swirled in the air, settling into the cracks of reality.

In coffee shops and living rooms across the nation, the discussions began, each hyperbolic promise echoing through the minds of voters like a catchy jingle that no longer felt pleasing. "He said what?" became the refrain as they replayed every outrageous statement, realizing how expertly they'd been led down the rabbit hole of comedy.

The absurdity reached its peak when a local group organized a 'Disillusionment Parade,' with floats decorated in the façades of Grindle's whimsical visions. "All aboard the 'Promises Train'," they chanted, as participants danced in oversized paper-mâché representations of Grindle's most outrageous claims, underscoring the farce with every exaggerated step.

Yet, amidst the laughter and gallows humor, an uncomfortable truth lingered. The realization that they'd been both the audience and the unwitting stars of this tragicomedy stirred an undercurrent of tension. The laughter, once filled with jovial camaraderie, now held the tremor of a shared reckoning—a hunger for clarity in the wasteland of their political naivety.

The town square turned electric with spontaneous debates as citizens grappled with their own gullibility. "How could we fall for such theatrics?" one questioned, laughter mingling with the disbelief that painted their cheeks a rosy hue. Yet another, a particularly passionate follower of the former savior, waved off the scrutiny with a nervous chuckle, too afraid to confront the abyss of disappointment that loomed ahead.

As the parade wound down, the atmosphere shifted into one charged with an odd mix of remaining loyalty and burgeoning dissent. It was the calm before the storm; beneath the jovial remarks, a pulse of rebellion simmered. Voters, once unified in enthusiasm, began to fracture, each split revealing deeper fractures in a society hungry for accountability.

In the shadow of Grindle's grand delusions, a pivotal moment was brewing. The laughter that had once shielded them now served as the irony of their awakening—an awakening that promised to be as bewildering as it was cathartic. The echoes of their laughter transformed into murmurs of rebellion, leaving everyone to wonder what would happen when the final curtain dropped on Grindle's comedy of errors.

Thus began the Great Disillusionment, not merely a surrender to reality, but an uproarious uprising against the absurdity that had robbed them of reason. Would they rise from the ashes of deception, or would they allow themselves to become repeat stars in this never-ending farce?

Subtle Undercurrents of Rebellion

The Awakening of the Complacent

In the heart of the city, where hope had once danced lightly on the whims of Gerald Grindle's promises, a subtle shift began to stir. Citizens who had spent the last few years entrenched in a soft haze of admiration for the charismatic leader found themselves blinking in disbelief. The vibrant murals of optimism that had plastered the walls began to crack, revealing the grayness beneath. It was as if a long nap had ended, and the groggy populace was beginning to realize they were not, in fact, living in a fairytale but rather in a comedic tragedy directed by a fool.

As the first notes of dissent started whispering through the cafés and street corners, conversations turned from idle chatter about the next grand spectacle Grindle promised to deliver to a flickering recognition of the absurdity that surrounded them. The collective epiphany was as electrifying as a jolt of caffeine to those who had slept through the last few seasons of political pandemonium. They began to share laughter—an irregular, contagious kind that bubbled up, infusing the air with a kind of defiance no one had expected to feel.

Yet, such awareness didn't come without its challenges. For some, the awakening was akin to removing a blindfold only to discover they had been riding a rollercoaster designed by a lunatic. Uncontrollable chuckles intermingled with gasps of horror as the faithful began recounting their encounters with Grindle's bizarre promises, once deemed brilliant, now appearing utterly ludicrous. Complacency shifted into rebellion, laughter mingled with incredulity, and a fierce resolve began to brew. It was a delicious irony: they had all been so blindly enslaved by Grindle's empty promises that now, in cascading waves of realization, freedom began to taste sweeter than any illusion of grandeur.

Mockery as a Form of Protest

As the air thickened with the stench of broken promises, the citizens began to stir. No longer the naive admirers of Gerald Grindle's grand proclamations, they found themselves in a state of awakening. What was once a misguided infatuation transformed into a bubbling cauldron of resentment. They gathered in makeshift assemblies, each one eager to share their stories of dashed hopes wrapped in the tinsel of Grindle's charm.

Out amongst them, those most adept in the art of mockery rose to prominence. They took to social media like fish to water, crafting scathing memes and biting satire that skewered Grindle's absurd assurances.

"Remember when he promised us unicorns? Well, here's your unicorn!" one exclaimed, sharing a hilariously poorly-drawn image of an actual horse with a glittery horn glued to its forehead. The laughter that erupted was as freeing as it was healing. Grindle's promises became a joke, and the populace didn't just find humor—they found power in ridicule.

As the wave of mockery gained momentum, it pulled in all sorts: the disillusioned, the sideways thinkers, and those who had just a little too much time on their hands. They became self-proclaimed 'Grindle's Clowns,' parading around in garish outfits adorned with his slogans, turning rallies into sideshows. The more Grindle floundered in his responses, the more inventive the jests became. What began as a subtle undercurrent of rebellion transformed into a full-blown carnival of dissent, complete with makeshift floats, derisive puppets, and nonsensical chants that echoed through the streets. Who knew humor could act as the grappling hook for the disenchanted souls of the electorate?

But as laughter filled the air, shadows crept closer. The more dissent the mockery sowed, the more desperate Grindle became. His zany solutions and whimsical promises faced a barrage of ridicule, but he responded not with reason, but with anger. His followers who once laughed amidst the absurd could feel the tide turning. The tension grew as whispers of retaliation echoed among the once-complacent. Would Grindle's regime respond with laughter or with a darkness that could suffocate their newly found voices?

The Rise of the Independent Thinker

As the campaigns rolled on, a tremor spread through the ranks of Grindle's once-adoring public. They were, after all, the people who had loudly proclaimed his name, who had danced in the aisles of his raucous rallies, now waking to the persistent itch of a thought too long repressed: could it be that they had been duped by a man dressed in nothing but a snazzy suit and a grin that could charm the scales off a crocodile?

Theirs was a collective awakening, a gradual shedding of the heavy cloak of complacency they had draped around their shoulders. The air crackled with a different static now—one that hummed of rebellion. They began to sniff the telltale signs of staleness in Grindle's charm, like yesterday's popcorn at a bad movie—unappetizing and easily discarded. It was the rise of the independent thinker, and they were armed with nothing but wit and some sharp-tipped pencils, ready to pen their truth.

Independent thinkers emerged as the real protagonists in this grand comedy, wielding clarity like a chef's finest knife, slicing through Grindle's abstraction with surgical precision. They laughed with abandon as they dissected the absurdity of promises that were more like balloon animals—intriguing at first glance but entirely deflated upon closer inspection. They had not only found their voice; they had found their sense of humor too!

In cozy coffee shops, they gathered to share their revelations, huddled over cups that steamed like their newly ignited passions. Did you hear Grindle promises a unicorn for every family? one would quip, with a smirk that suggested a deeper truth beneath the laughter. Another would chime in, Right, but only if you pay your taxes in glitter! It was a cacophony of absurdity turned into a rallying cry, a mutual recognition that the greatest weapon they now possessed was their ability to laugh in the face of rhetoric.

With every snicker, the chains of prior indignation loosened, revealing the powerful elasticity of independent thought. These thinkers began to question the very fabric of Grindle's theatrics, and they were not alone. Citizens once dazzled by Grindle's glimmering promises slowly began to realize that their loyalty, much like a rubber band, could stretch but not break, and they were ready to snap back with a vengeance.

Yet, the audacity it took to stand against such persuasive prowess brewed tension like a storm cloud hanging low over an unsuspecting landscape. The imminent conflict between Grindle's glittering façade and the raw honesty of the independent thinkers was brewing, promising fireworks that could light up the entire political arena. But as they gathered their resolve, the shadow of Grindle's charisma loomed larger, and one question echoed louder than the rest: Would laughter truly triumph over the guise of confidence, or was a retaliatory force brewing beneath the surface?

A Comedic Interlude

The Art of Sarcasm

Sarcasm served as a delightful weapon for dissenters, cutting through the fog of Gerald Grindle's absurd leadership with wit sharper than a double-edged sword. As Grindle's promises floated in the air like helium balloons – colorful but ultimately deflating – the skeptics emerged armed with quips and jabs that made even the most steadfast supporters chuckle in self-doubt.

In the coffee shops and cafes where loyalists gathered, a new form of camaraderie emerged, forged in the fires of shared mockery. "Oh, look! Another shiny promise from Saint Gerald! Shall we hang it on our vision board next to last week's 'moon colonies by 2025' announcement?" A riotous laughter often cropped up among those who could finally see through the smoke and mirrors. Laughter became not just a coping mechanism, but an unsanctioned rallying cry against the absurdity they had once celebrated.

Meanwhile, on social media, the insanity escalated into a boundless playground for memes and one-liners that transformed Grindle's ludicrous declarations into punchlines that spread faster than his empty rhetoric. As citizens plunged into this whimsical world of sarcasm, a seismic shift began; people started contemplating the magnitude of their prior belief in a leader who seemed to spin ridiculous tales rather than govern. This churning tide of realization grew more intense, pulling everyone closer to a moment of collective awakening—even within the most staunchly loyal who realized they had perhaps misread the map of their faith.

Laughter as a Weapon

In the midst of chaos, laughter echoed like a defiant battle cry, weaving through the streets and alleyways where citizens found their voices amid the absurdity of Grindle's grand promises. In coffee shops, parks, and even in the confines of urban apartments, disillusioned supporters began to gather, dusting off their humor like an old, cherished blanket. Sarcasm became their shield, an ironclad armor against the relentless barrage of empty rhetoric and false hope.

A group of dissenters discovered that the sharp edge of wit could pierce the thick veil of delusion shrouding Grindle's followers. They gathered in secret, whispering jokes and crafting clever jabs that painted Grindle not as their savior but as a bumbling fool, continuously tripping over his own words and miscalculations. With every laugh, they recognized their resilience growing, transforming despair into a vibrant tapestry of humor that bound them together against the tide of political naiveté.

As the days went on, their laughter became contagious, rippling through the masses, each chuckle straining against the silence of compliance. The city was lit with an electrifying energy—jokesters began turning Grindle's gaffes into comedic gold, sharing memes and illustrations that made their rounds online. With each share, they dismantled Grindle's facade piece by piece, revealing the tragicomedy of his leadership to all who had laughed along with them. But just as they basked in the glow of their newfound unity, the question loomed: would laughter be enough to awaken their fellow citizens from their slumber, or would the punchlines fizzle out in the face of an unyielding farce?

Cartoon Politics: A Doodle of Dissent

In an age where reality often feels stranger than fiction, the realm of cartoons flourishes as a refuge for those grappling with the absurdity of Grindle's administration. Political satire transforms the airwaves into a vibrant canvas where dissent finds voice through exaggerated caricatures and witty narratives. Every editorial illustrates Grindle's escapades as both a clown and a jester, mocking his overblown promises with a cheeky smile. Amidst the colors, the laughter becomes a resilient form of protest, creativity escaping the constraints of a world gone mad.

As satirical animators skewer Grindle's misguided policies, the populace discovers a respite within these doodles. Each cartoon features Grindle's iconic smile, juxtaposed against the wreckage of his promises: flying pigs to symbolize his fantastical economic growth and a basket of empty promises tumbling from his hands, much to the amusement of bemused viewers. The laughter, undeniable and contagious, spreads through neighborhoods like wildfire, igniting conversations at coffee shops, playgrounds, and barstools alike, encouraging the once-complacent to re-evaluate their loyalties and laugh at their former naiveté.

Yet, as the ink dries on these whimsical sketches, there lingers an undercurrent of tension. The absurdity that brought joy now subtly morphs into a rallying cry—a call to arms hidden within the laughter. Citizens begin to grasp that humor does not merely serve to relieve their despair; it serves to wake them up. In the twisted unveiling of Grindle's mishaps, a cartoon revolution brews, as forbidden thoughts slide through the barrier of collective compliance. The doodles hold the potential to spark rebellion, each funny frame encapsulating a truth long obscured by Grindle's glittering facade. With every stroke of the pen, the absurdity tightens, leading them to question how much longer they can bear the weight of their overlord's comedic tyranny.

The Tipping Point

THE TIPING POINT

GERLD GRINDLE

DESPESLE MEASEURES

Media backlash ignites awareness, and citizens humorously question their blind admiration. As journalists don their capes, they dive into the fray with the fervor of caffeinated squirrels, armed with cameras and sarcasm. Headlines blare like sirens, each more outrageous than the last, as reports of Gerald Grindle's escapades fall into the public eye like confetti at a poorly planned parade. The charming savior, once revered, now faces the relentless spotlight of critical scrutiny.

Cynicism seeps into the consciousness of the once-gleeful supporters, who stand as if caught in a surprise rain shower, laughter mingling with disbelief. "Did we really believe he could fix everything with a dance routine and a sack of promises?" one citizen quips, peeling away the layers of absurdity from their past adoration. The media dishes out the dirt, seasoning it with wit, showcasing the hilarity of Grindle's antics with relish. The shift in sentiment is palpable, akin to a dramatic plot twist in a long-running sitcom—the applause from the audience begins to wane.

As whistleblowers emerge, blending into the crowd like undercover agents in the midst of a heist, humorous truth-telling antics highlight the farcical nature of Grindle's grand illusions. "You call that leadership? My grandmother could do better with a bingo paddle!" shouts a disgruntled reporter during a live broadcast, inadvertently inspiring a new trend in mockery. Sensing the tide turning, Grindle's followers try to defend their beloved leader, but their arguments sound less like passionate convictions and more like someone trying to convince themselves that a burnt meal is gourmet. Coherent thoughts stagger under the weight of absurdity, as the audience watches, slack-jawed and giggling.

As the facade begins to crumble, the comedic chaos unfurls—a joyful frenzy of reactions cascades through the populace. Each report brings fresh laughter, each revelation a dose of clarity intertwined with comedic irony that highlights the pitfalls of once-deaf loyalty. Really, was it worth trading rational thought for a rollercoaster ride of ridiculous hopes? The audience huddles together in shared disbelief, feeling lighter with each chuckle, all the while preparing for the next wave of revelations as their society precariously teeters on the brink of delightful mayhem.

Whistleblowers in Disguise

In the midst of Grindle's chaotic charade, a peculiar faction began to emerge, unnoticed by the adoring crowds who were too busy sipping the Kool-Aid. These were the comic whistleblowers, armed not with legal pads or briefcases, but rather with rubber chickens and oversized glasses. They donned the guise of loyal followers while secretly plotting to reveal the absurdity that fueled Grindle's reign of nonsense.

With a flair for the dramatic and a penchant for the ridiculous, they infiltrated rallies, crafting elaborate tales of speculative truths that turned Grindle's promises into punchlines. One whistleblower, who styled himself as 'The Truthinator,' managed to sway the audience's laughter as he paraded around in a chicken suit, crowing out the absurdities woven into Grindle's rhetoric. Laughter erupted, but behind the facade, a message was steadily emerging, paving the way for an explosion of awareness.

As these unlikely truth-tellers took center stage, the tides began to shift. Citizens who once idolized Grindle started nudging each other in confusion, sensing that beneath the humor lay a kernel of reality too absurd to ignore. The Truthinator's antics transformed from mere entertainment to a catalyst for thought, igniting a slow-burning flame of skepticism in the hearts of the formerly zealous supporters. The stage was set for a comical uprising, where humor would blend with revelation, and the laughter heard during Grindle's rallies became a terrifying echo of self-awareness.

When the Walls Start to Crumble

As Gerald Grindle's carefully constructed facade began to show signs of strain, citizens found themselves both amused and bewildered by the absurdity unfolding around them. The charismatic savior who once promised them a golden future was now entangled in a web of his own convoluted lies, making even the most hopeful follower question their blind faith. It was as if the universe was hosting a grand comedy show, with Grindle's missteps serving as the punchlines that had everyone chuckling, even as they rolled their eyes in disbelief.

Suddenly, whispers of doubt echoed in towns and cities. The once adoring crowds began to parse through Grindle's soundbites, like keen detectives scrutinizing a suspect's alibi. Citizens chuckled as they recalled his outlandish claims, "A spaceship in every garage!" and "Magical gardens that grow money!" They started to question—was there ever a real plan behind the razzle-dazzle, or was it merely a magician's illusion? The more they rummaged through their memories, the more they found themselves torn between nostalgia for the mirage of hope and the gritty reality that lurked beneath.

Meanwhile, the media—a character of its own in this farcical narrative—decided it was time to turn up the heat. With headlines screaming every minor misstep, they portrayed Grindle's governance as an epic sitcom where the laughs stemmed from sheer disbelief. As the media circus amplified, citizens began to embrace the absurdity, sharing memes and jokes online that depicted Grindle as a lovable yet bumbling fool. The more the walls of his charade cracked, the more the laughter echoed through the streets, casting a surreal yet unifying spell over the disillusioned populace.

Then came the whistleblowers, those brave few in ill-fitting costumes, who decided to step into the limelight. With comedic flair, they revealed one ludicrous truth after another—"Did you know Grindle's 'green energy' plan involved nothing more than a leaf blower?" They danced across stages, waving ridiculously fabricated documents that humorously highlighted just how deep the charade ran. The air was thick with a mix of embarrassment and laughter as they stripped away the glamorous veneer, exposing the reality beneath like peeling paint from a shabby wall.

As the truths began to emerge, the followers who once viewed Grindle as a prophet of prosperity now stood in shock, caught between laughter and denial. "Surely, he didn't mean it like that!" a devoted follower gasped, clinging to the vestiges of belief as their fellow citizens erupted into fits of laughter at the unfolding absurdity.

Each revelation was met with gasps followed by guffaws as audiences shifted from seeing their leader as a savior to recognizing the farce that had been leading them to ruin.

With Grindle's carefully curated image in tatters, the walls of delusion crumbled further, revealing the underlying absurdity of their blind loyalty. As the laughter echoed, it morphed from mere amusement into something more—an awakening. The citizens began to comprehend that while they may have laughed at Grindle's antics, it was their own complicity they had to confront. What would they do now in this chaotic landscape, both humorous and tragic? The tension built, for the final reveal was looming. Would they laugh together, or was their laughter merely a prelude to a sobering realization that their very foundation had been built on empty rhetoric and grand illusions?

The Final Confrontation

The Night of Reckoning

Voters gathered under the flickering streetlights, an electrified crowd more akin to a stand-up comedy show than a political rally. Whispers of disbelief mingled with laughter as Gerald Grindle emerged from his chauffeur-driven chariot, a makeshift altar of outrageous promises towering beside him like a cardboard castle threatened by a gentle breeze.

"Ladies and gentlemen!" he proclaimed in a voice thick with false enthusiasm, "Tonight, my friends, I stand before you not merely as a candidate, but as your Savior-in-Chief! Let's have a round of applause for the glorious train wreck that has been our last term!" His self-deprecating humor was met with raucous laughter, but beneath the chuckles lay the tightening rope of discontent that had slowly wove itself into the very fabric of the gathering.

As the moon shone down like a spotlight, the air crackled with anticipation and a hint of rebellion. Mock signs reading "More Hot Air, Less Hot Water!" waved vigorously among the crowd. In the back, a group of indignant citizens began circulating a video montage where Grindle's promises were juxtaposed against images of collapsed bridges and runaway inflation, a feast of irony seasoned with escalating absurdity.

With an exaggerated flourish, Grindle pulled out a giant scroll that declared his latest slew of promises, a poetic disaster penned in glittering gold. "Fear not, for I will solve crime with free ice cream and engage our youth with mandatory mime classes!" His followers cheered, but the snickers among others grew louder, blossoming into full guffaws as the truth began to tiptoe into view. Each outrageous assertion sparked another wave of disbelief, adding to the growing crescendo of mockery.

Just then, a whistle pierced the air, cutting through the jovial facade. A previously overlooked citizen, armed only with a digital tablet and an unyielding spirit, rallied forth with television-anchored confidence. "Grindle! You call that a plan? I've seen better plots in a soap opera!" The crowd gasped, half in shock, half in delight, as the challenger grabbed the mic and launched into a captivating, yet humorous, litany of Grindle's past blunders, transforming his campaign pitch into a roast that had people spilling their nachos with laughter.

Suddenly, all eyes were on Grindle, the glimmer of sweat appearing on his brow—a contagion of doubt wafting through his meticulously crafted facade. "But... but..." he stammered, a deer caught in the headlights of reality. You could almost hear the gears grinding in his head, the once-tuned rhetoric now misfiring into an array of comedic chaos. The tide was shifting, laughter turned into a weapon, and Grindle was slowly becoming the butt of the cosmic joke he had initiated.

With the audience rising like a tide, laughter rode the surging wave of rebellion, builds peaking as Grindle's earlier bravado dwindled, transforming him from a charismatic showman to a punchline desperate to rewrite the script. "Remember folks, change is possible," he quipped nervously, "with courage, creativity, and… perhaps a really impactful PowerPoint presentation?" The crowd erupted in laughter, half cheering, half jeering, a beautiful symphony of civic discontent and hopeful absurdity hanging thick in the air.

It was evident—the night would not end in glory for Grindle, but rather in the upheaval of carefully crafted delusions, each laugh a nail in the coffin of his floundering farce. The tipping point was here, and the clock was ticking as the moon bore witness to the farcical showdown, the final chapter of Grindle's comedy now almost too absurd to write.

The Revelation in Real-Time

As the atmosphere crackled with a mix of anticipation and absurdity, the scene unfolded like a bizarre circus performance. Voters, once enchanted by Gerald Grindle's loquacious charm, now crammed into the venue like sardines auditioning for a reality show titled Who Can Ignore the Elephant in the Room? The air was thick with a strange cocktail of hopeful anxiety and pungent realization.

Live on-air cameras broadcast the rally, capturing not just the spectacle but also the simmering tension among the audience. Grindle stood on stage, a somewhat absurd figure in an ill-fitting suit that seemed to shrink with each shaky breath he took, as if even the fabric wanted to escape the mess he'd created. "Ladies and gentlemen!" he bellowed, a mix of bravado and desperation dripping from his voice, "Tonight we unveil the grand designs of our future!" The collective groan echoed through the crowd, reminiscent of a symphony playing a note slightly off-key.

Just then, the unexpected happened—a stray microphone was accidentally left on, capturing snippets of whispered conversations among the crowd. "Did he really think we'd buy that last promise?" one woman stated, her brows furrowed in disbelief, while a man nearby chuckled, "I'd rather trust my crusty old cat with my life savings than Grindle!" Laughter erupted, and soon the entire audience was transformed into a chorus of humorous mutinies, riffing on the absurdities they'd been subjected to over the past few months.

Meanwhile, on the stage, Grindle's facade began to crack. The reality of his situation dawned on him amidst the laughter puncturing through his grandiosity. With each insult disguised as a joke, the growing awareness of his followers turned the event from a promising gala into a roast, turning his once trusty rhetoric into nothing more than bad punchlines. It was a public evisceration, and the reaction wasn't what he had hoped for; it spiraled into a roaring wave that threatened to drag him under like an anchor made of despair.

As Grindle grasped for control, he released a series of increasingly absurd promises—each one more ridiculous than the last, dripping with desperation. "I will implement a policy to give every citizen free puppies! Happiness will flow like rivers, and our economy will boom!" A wave of hysterical laughter rose like a tide of reality against the mediocre laughter that had preceded it. Grindle, now resembling a drowning man clutching at straws, spiraled into a parody of himself.

The crowd turned into an audience for a live comedy roast, and Grindle found himself at the mercy of unrelenting humor. At that moment, as cameras rolled and memes were born, he became an unwitting participant in a theatrical unveiling of incompetence. The stage was his, but the script had been rewritten by the very people he had sought to manipulate. Reality, once again, proved to be stranger—and funnier—than fiction.

A Showdown of Wit and Grit

The atmosphere buzzed with anticipation as the crowd gathered, eyes gleaming with the promise of confrontation. The stage was set, not for a mundane political spectacle, but for a showdown worthy of legend—a comedic duel where wit prepared to clash head-on with the bombastic rhetoric of Gerald Grindle.

Grindle, standing with an almost ridiculous grandeur, flashed his signature grin—a façade so polished that it could blind the casual observer. Ladies and gentlemen! he bellowed, "Tonight, I stand before you not just as a candidate, but as your chosen commander in this epic battle against the doldrums of reality!"

But deep within the throng, whispers of dissent rippled through like a dramatic wind. An independent thinker, armed only with a microphone and a razor-sharp tongue, stepped forward into the spotlight. "Commander?" he chuckled, "You mean commander-in-folly! Your promised land looks more like a circus tent collapsing under the weight of your own absurdity."

The crowd erupted, laughter filling the air, a tidal wave crashing against the shores of Grindle's bluster. Grindle's grin faltered for just a split second, and the audience savored the moment like fine wine. Rising to the occasion, he leaned into his bravado. "My good man, if my leadership is a circus, I am the ringmaster, orchestrating wonders beyond your timid imagination!"

This only fueled the independent thinker. "Oh, a ringmaster, indeed! But it seems all you're juggling are empty promises and rubber chickens!" The quip sent shockwaves of laughter through the crowd, amplifying the energy, the humor of the absurd crashing against Grindle's desperate attempts at seriousness.

As the banter intensified, a gaudy countdown timer appeared on the big screen, ticking down to the grand finale. The stakes were rising, and so were the spirits of the audience—who realized they might just be on the brink of something memorable.

Cup of coffee in hand, another member of the crowd couldn't help but chant, "Wit is winning! Wit is winning!" Grindle's eyes darted nervously; he had built an empire atop the quicksand of his own words, and now it was all precariously toppling down with each punchline thrown like arrows toward his inflated ego.

In the midst of the clash, Grindle's tone shifted. "You think you can dismantle my truths with mere jabs? I shall reveal the magic of my vision!" But the audience knew better, and the air crackled with humorous disbelief. They were there, not just with mockery, but with a lingering hunger for liberation from the absurdity that had woven around their lives.

As the countdown dwindled down, tension reached a peak, and with it, the playful absurdity transformed into a serious realm of introspection. Laughter, once a weapon of the independent thinker, now painted a backdrop for realization; the joke was on them all, yet here they were, united in a quest for clarity beneath the comedic ruse.

And just at the split second before the timer hit zero, an unexpected gasp rippled through the audience—what if Grindle's insults weren't simply bluster, but the very essence of the folly they had followed blindly? The reckoning loomed as the spotlight divided the stage, illuminating the surreal spectacle of wit battling the guile of a once-beloved savior. The audience held their breath, knowing the saga of absurdity was about to take a revolutionary turn.

The Aftermath: A New Reality

The Dust Settles

In the wake of Gerald Grindle's exit from the stage, the citizens awakened from their collective stupor, blinking like owls at the harsh light of reality. They gathered in small groups, swapping tales that were comically embellished in the retelling, tales of promises unfulfilled and mirages that evaporated the moment they dared to reach for them. A mother recounted how Grindle's promised free ice cream turned out to be a mere smear of whipped cream on a single, melted scoop. A neighbor chimed in with a story of a rally where Grindle had raised his hand dramatically, vowing to cure all ailments with a sprinkle of his 'magic solution'—an unbranded bottle of soda that sold out minutes after the claim. The humor spun from their absurd experiences offered a balm for the scars left by blind loyalty.

As laughter echoed through the streets, it slowly morphed into a shared realization: they had been more than just victims; they were unwitting participants in a grand comedy. The acceptance of their gullibility brought a new kind of freedom, a fresh air after being buried in a cloud of hot air for so long. "What will we do now?" one citizen mused, half-jokingly suggesting a festival celebrating the Great Grindle Debacle, where they could reenact his speeches complete with theatrics and exaggerated accents. The mere thought unraveled more giggles, hinting at a collective healing process.

But as the humor took root, a tangible tension began to weave itself into their conversations. A subplot developed around a smattering of dissenters who quietly gathered in corners, whispering of the necessity to hold Grindle accountable—not with spite, but with a glint of mischief. "We've lost too much—let's flip this script on his promises. What if we start tallying how many ludicrous claims he made? That could be our next performance!" they declared with fervor. A complicated map of emotions emerged as some citizens clung to nostalgia for the absurdity while others sought to dismantle it, their friendly banter morphing into an unspoken competition. Whose betrayal hurt the most? As the dust settled, they found themselves caught in a pledge that hanging onto the past could either doom them to repeat it or lead to a renaissance of reason. From laughter to tension, the room filled with the realization that a change was coming, whether it was wanted or not.

A Change of Heart or a Change of Tide?

In the wake of Gerald Grindle's whimsical reign, the citizens of this absurd reality gathered in cafes, pubs, and community halls, each clinking their mugs filled with something stronger than coffee, as they reminisced about their blind adoration. Laughter and disbelief mingled like odd dance partners in a crowded room, where once a blind loyalty stood firm. As they exchanged tales of their past fervor, a flicker of rebellion began to spark.

"I mean, remember when we thought he could solve our problems with a smile and a magic wand?" one citizen quipped, her voice laced with disbelief. "He promised us the moon, yet we barely got discounts on parking tickets." The collective chuckle reflected a growing sense of clarity—the kind that creeps in when you realize the joke has been on you all along. Yet there lingered a faint sense of loyalty, like trying to keep a balloon afloat with no air in it.

As discussions grew murkier and debates raged on, the question loomed large: Was it time to forgive the man who painted delusions on the canvas of governance? Some argued vehemently that perhaps a change of heart was due—after all, who hasn't made a poor choice before? Others countered with a wave of sarcasm that rippled through the room, "Forgive him? I wouldn't trust him to bring me an umbrella if I was standing in a rainstorm!"

The air buzzed with tension as opinions clashed, akin to a circus without a ringmaster. Some sought to free themselves from the shackles of loyalty, while others were still enchanted by the glittering promises. It was a comedic tug-of-war that echoed through the streets, with citizens either laughing at their own folly or fighting to reclaim their misguided devotion. In this chaotic sea of emotions, the tides of change began to shift, hinting at a raucous storm brewing on the horizon.

Yet as the humor thickened, so did the realization that this could very well be a pivotal moment; a change not just of heart, but of tide. Citizens found themselves at a crossroads, poised between the hilarity of their past gullibility and the potential for an enlightened future. Was it time to toss aside the remnants of their worn loyalty, or embrace the absurdity with a laugh? The debate raged on, each moment thick with anticipation, leading them inadvertently towards a reckoning that promised to be just as hilariously chaotic as Gerald Grindle's brief, shiny era.

Rhetoric Revisited: Lessons Learned Too Late

In the aftermath of Gerald Grindle's chaos, a newfound clarity swept over the citizens like a cold breeze through an open window. They gathered in cafes and living rooms, narrating their outrageous tales as if recounting the daftest sitcom episode. Each story morphed into an absurd masterpiece, layered with the ridiculousness of their past beliefs. "Remember when he promised us flying cars?" one chuckled, waving his hands animatedly. Laughter erupted, punctuated by the strange realization that the promise of personal jetpacks had been mere hyperbole, much like everything else that had ever dribbled from Grindle's mouth.

As they swapped stories, a collective epiphany dawned; their previous blind loyalty mirrored the delusions of a group of cult members following a leader who hadn't even learned to juggle. The chatter turned from giggles to gasps as one citizen wondered aloud, "How did we let ourselves fall into this trap? Were all those flashy promises simply clever distractions?" The air thickened with an uncomfortable silence as the group wrestled with their own gullibility, each individual recalling the siren song of Grindle's rhetoric that had seemed so sweet once upon a time.

In the corners of the coffee shops, someone whispered, "What if we're just a punchline in Grindle's grand joke?" That bold notion shoved its way through the crowd like a rogue wave, earning nods of agreement and sensational bursts of laughter. But in that humor lurked a hint of trepidation, an acknowledgment that lessons learned too late can sting worse than a bee on a hot summer day. The absurdity of their predicament washed over them, stirring a mixture of embarrassment and amusement that felt all too familiar. And so, they raised their mugs high, toasting not to their fallen leader but to their newfound clarity—one steeped in hilarity yet hauntingly serious.

Building the Future: Trojan Horse Style

Innovations Born from Necessity

As chaos reigned supreme in the aftermath of Grindle's political antics, the creative juices of the citizens began to flow like cheap wine at a questionable wedding. What arose from the pandemonium was a series of absurd innovations, each a humorous reflection of the desperate times. Local inventors, inspired by the chaos, crafted the Bureaucracy Blaster—a comically large contraption meant to streamline the endless forms and paperwork that had become synonymous with governmental processes. Of course, all it did was shoot out confetti and streamers every time someone turned in a new document, but the joy it brought was unquantifiable, drowning out the dreariness of bureaucracy.

Meanwhile, the younger generation, fueled by a paradoxical mix of skepticism and hope, huddled around makeshift tables with duct tape and dreams, devising the first-ever Rhetorical Regret Detector. This whimsical invention was a small box adorned with blinking lights and funny sounds, programmed to alert its user whenever a politician was speaking—especially if the words came dipped in honeyed promises. The catch? It only worked when someone uttered the phrase "trust me," triggering a cacophony of alarms and exaggerated comedic gasps.

In community centers, adults and children alike gathered for workshops on how to transform disappointment into laughter, learning to craft pithy slogans and absurd memes to mock the political farce they found themselves ensnared in. We're all just one punchline away from freedom! became a rallying cry of sorts, echoing through the streets. Amidst this whirlwind of creativity, tension simmered just below the surface; would Grindle's reign be met with mere ridicule, or could these innovations forge a path towards genuine awareness?

Reaching for the Stars Beneath the Lies

In a whimsical whirlwind of chaos and confusion, citizens began to grasp the absurdity of their situation. They realized that beneath Grindle's captivating charm lay a sea of fabrications as vast as the sky they yearned to reach. Reluctantly, they started to sift through the layers of deception that had clouded their judgment, much like archaeologists unearthing forgotten relics in a landscape of political ruins.

As they stumbled upon truths disguised as laughter, people began to craft their own constellations of understanding. Each chuckle and snicker transformed into stars, illuminating the darkness that Grindle had cast over their minds. Like poorly drawn cartoons come to life, these moments of clarity inspired them to reach for something more meaningful than hollow promises, chipping away at the concrete spells woven around their thoughts.

In the comedic uproar of their collective awakening, parody became their shield, laughter their weapon. They shared inside jokes about Grindle's circus acts, uniting in a hilarity that transcended the madness of their reality. Yet, as the bubbling humor rose to the surface, an unsettling tension brewed beneath; people found themselves caught between the comforting lies they had once clung to and the liberating truths that beckoned them forward.

With pens in hand and spontaneous wit sparking in their minds, they began to document their odyssey through absurdity, crafting a script for a future that no longer included Grindle's whimsical touch. But would they have the courage to fully embrace this newfound truth? The stakes had never been higher, and the unanswered question loomed over them: could they truly reach for the stars without the net of deception that had once held them captive?

Healing Through Humor

As the dust began to settle in the chaotic whirlwind left behind by Grindle, laughter became a secret language among those who had once been deceived. What better therapy for a collective heartbreak than a hearty laugh? Communities gathered around rusted park benches, where stories of woe transformed into comedies of errors, bridging gaps between friends and former foes alike.

Local comedians took to the streets, wearing unflattering wigs and exaggerated suits reminiscent of the man they once trusted. "Have you heard the one about the politician who promised everyone a unicorn? Turns out it was just a horse with a party hat!" The humor exacerbated the absurd, bringing stifled chuckles to the masses, who suddenly realized the shared folly of their blind faith.

In this tapestry of resilience, amidst the echoes of laughter, healing found a foothold. Neighborhoods began hosting "Grindle Roast" nights, where citizens could candidly air their grievances through satire, poking fun at their own gullibility and recognizing the layers of manipulation they had unwittingly accepted. Through punchlines and puns, unity blossomed, while the shadows of deceit slowly receded.

Yet, as the laughter rang loud, a deeper tension brewed—where would the healing journey lead next? The very fabric of this newfound camaraderie was stitched with threads of skepticism, and questions loomed like a dark cloud over their collective heads. Would they be able to harness this humor as a weapon against future deceivers? Or would they merely settle for giggles while forgetting the past too soon?

In the midst of chuckling children and grinning elders, the laughter morphed, reminding them that healing through humor was a double-edged sword. As the sun set behind the recovering town, one thing was clear: while humor might light the path to recovery, the lesson of vigilance loomed heavy as unwanted ink on a blank page. As they shared this newfound joy, whispers of hope and caution intertwined; after all, the past had taught them to expect the unexpected.

Encounters with the Enslaved Mind

Conversations Over Coffee

Encouners *with* the Inspired Mind

As the steam curled up from their mugs, the small café bustled with the energy of local patrons, but at a corner table, a different kind of energy simmered. Gerald Grindle's name hovered over the chatter like a raincloud poised to burst; it ignited laughter as much as it sparked ire. "Did you hear him say he's going to install golden sidewalks? What's next, a unicorn crossing guard?" chuckled Marge, her eyes dancing as she took a sip of her cappuccino.

Her companion, Dave, rolled his eyes, but a smile crept onto his face. "Yeah, and all the potholes will be filled with whipped cream! It's like he thinks we're still in kindergarten. Next, he'll promise ice cream for all and call it a day." The table erupted in laughter, their jokes spinning wild tales of Grindle's ever-inflating promises, each more ridiculous than the last, bonding them over the shared absurdity of it all.

Yet beneath the levity, a disquieting awareness began bubbling to the surface. "But seriously," Dave interjected, his voice lowering as if to shield the thought from the very walls of the café. "What if people actually believe him? I mean, we chuckle now, but doesn't that just make us part of the problem? Are we really going to continue sipping our lattes while he's busy making a mockery of us?" The laughter faded, the weight of those words hanging uncomfortably in the air, a premonition ballooning between them.

Marge stared into her cup, swirling its remnants. "You think it's too late? That we're too far gone? I mean, to be fair, it's not like we aren't entertained. It's like watching a circus – you know it's a mess, but you can't look away." Her attempt to brush off the gravity fell flat, and silence enveloped the table, an aching juxtaposition to their earlier mirth.

As the minutes ticked by, anxiety and amusement crashed against each other, building a tension that could no longer be ignored. "What if we're the show?" Dave whispered, half-serious, half-joking. "What if we're the audience cheering on the clowns as they juggle our futures?"

In that moment, clarity struck, slicing through the laughter like a knife. They weren't merely spectators; they were participants tangled in the fabric of Grindle's farce. Marge's eyes sparkled with a flicker of rebellious recognition. "Then maybe it's time we stop being the audience. Maybe we need to get off this bleacher and write our own script." The idea hung in the air, crackling with potential.

With their certainty solidifying, the pair felt an unexpected exhilaration brewing—a burgeoning rebellion fueled by caffeine and camaraderie, an awakening from the stupor of mindless entertainment. They clinked their mugs together, a toast not just to coffee but to the stirring realization that within their laughter, there lay the seeds of change.

Breaking the Chains: Voices of Reason

Over the clinking of mugs and the aroma of brewing coffee, laughter erupted like popcorn in a hot pan. Ellen and Mark, nestled at their favorite café, shared stories that sparkled with absurdity. They chuckled over the ludicrous promises of their once-beloved political savior, Gerald Grindle, whose every vow seemed crafted in a whimsy factory for the hopelessly optimistic. "Remember when he claimed he'd eliminate taxes? I half expected him to pull a rabbit out of a hat!" Ellen exclaimed, her voice light with humor.

As the coffee flowed, seeds of reason took root amidst the laughter. "But really, Ellen, how did we fall for it?" Mark pondered, a playful smirk illuminating his face. "He had us convinced that following the absurd was the key to prosperity, and here we are with empty wallets and full mugs!" The camaraderie morphed their shared folly into a source of amusement, creating a safe space for the absurdities of allegiance that held them captive.

Then, as if struck by lightning, their laughter turned serious. "You know, it's frightening how easily we surrendered our minds," Ellen whispered, a gravity settling over the table like a heavy blanket. "But what if we just… stopped?" Mark leaned closer, excitement swirling in his eyes. "Imagine if we broke these chains of thought! What if we dared to think for ourselves?" With that simple question, an electric tension crackled in the air. Each realized that beneath the humor lay a potent truth, and they stood at the precipice of awakening filled with anticipation of what lay beyond the absurdity.

The Awakening Spark!

Over a steaming cup of coffee, the absurdities of Grindle's reign spilled out with each chuckle, as friends gathered to exchange tales of misplaced loyalty. Barry, with a twinkle in his eye, recounted the time he believed Grindle's promise to turn the town fountain into a sparkling waterfall of prosperity. The image of taxpayers funding a fountain that never worked had them all in stitches, yet beneath the laughter lay an unsettling realization—a bond of absurdity had tethered them to his fanciful claims.

As the laughter faded, lively discussions hinted at the awakening of reason. Jane raised a brow and quipped, Isn't blindly following Grindle like dating a magician? It's all tricks and no substance. Chiming in, Tom added with a grin, Exactly! We might as well be juggling lobsters at a barbecue! The only way to break free from this circus is to let the truth snap those chains. The collective mirth sparked a new energy, one of clarity hidden under layers of comedic absurdity.

Then, out of the blue, Clara erupted with a wild notion, What if we start a club? The Independent Thinkers Society! We can wear logic like a badge of honor—and perhaps some zany hats for flair! Initially met with laughter, her suggestion ignited a sense of excitement; it was their very own awakening spark. Who knew silliness could be the cradle of critical thought? As plans began to form, they felt something shift—a flicker of freedom slowly replacing the haze of political enchantment.

The Election: A Finale in Theatrical Style

Curtains Up! The Grand Finale

As the countdown to the election results commenced, anticipation crackled in the air like static electricity before a storm. Citizens gathered in droves, eyes glued to their screens, as if their very futures hinged on the antics of Gerald Grindle. Confetti flew, music blared, and cheerleaders with pom-poms danced in a frenzy, transforming the dull precinct into a carnival of chaos.

All the over-the-top pageantry was an ode to the absurdity of an election that had, in many ways, outstripped the creative boundaries of the imagination. Yet in the midst of the revelry, a sense of dread simmered below the surface—would this be the day that voters finally opened their eyes, or were they merely inches away from enjoying yet another round of Grindle's whimsical concoctions?

As the clock hit midnight, the results began to flash on the screen, punctuating the air with a dramatic flair. Cheers erupted when Grindle's name lit up the scoreboard, followed by a collective gasp that echoed throughout the crowd. Was that laughter or the crunch of disbelief? Faces twisted in melodrama as supporters danced in ecstasy, while skeptics clutched each other, peering from the corners of their eyes, fervently searching for hidden meaning behind the flashing numbers.

Suddenly, the emcee, resplendent in sequins, announced a surprise performance—Grindle himself would take the stage to deliver an acceptance speech that promised to be as fantastical as a Broadway show. The absurdity was palpable; it felt as if reality had taken a back seat to theatricality.

He stepped up, donning a top hat and a sparkly jacket, gliding across the stage like a magician poised to pull a rabbit from a hat. Dearest constituents, he began, "tonight is not just about me; it's about you, the loyal believers in a world of impossibilities!" Laughter bubbled up, an involuntary reaction to the sheer ridiculousness of it all. Would they truly buy what he was selling, even as they gagged on the taste of it?

As Grindle spun tales of promise and dreams, a strange mixture of charm and insanity enveloped the room. The crescendo of the moment approached its pinnacle, and just as the citizens thought they were caught up in a classic political melodrama, a different act began to unfold. Dissenters wielding banners began to emerge from the shadows, throwing metaphorical tomatoes—from all angles, the tension mounted.

In a twist befitting a Greek tragedy, Grindle's whimsical charm began to weaken. His minions faltered while laughter began to morph into the sound of a collective snicker. Rebellion bubbled beneath the laughter, as the absurd show began to unravel in a flurry of accusations, counterclaims, and comedic irony.

As the curtains prepared to drop on this chaotic spectacle, the crowd split between followers and skeptics, laughter mingling with tension, creating an electric atmosphere fraught with uncertain resolution. The question lingered: in the impending silence, who would emerge victorious from this grand finale—Grindle and his absurd kingdom or the awakened citizens, ready to reclaim their narrative with barbed humor and swiftly written reality checks?

Reactions and Reflections

The election results unfolded like an elaborate stage play, where the curtain rose to reveal a confused audience and a bewildered leading man. Citizens gathered around their screens and in living rooms, faces painted in a comedy of expressions ranging from disbelief to hysterical laughter. The grand finale was not just a political outcome; it was a theatrical spectacle of epic proportions.

As the results trickled in, laughter erupted, sometimes nervously, other times with genuine amusement. Did we really think he could pull it off? one citizen mused, swirling a cold drink that had long lost its chill. The absurdity of it all became a shared joke, as tales were spun about the promises that were as tangible as clouds. Each broken commitment felt like a slapstick gag, bringing moments of shared hilarity despite the looming stark reality.

In cafes and backyards, friends gathered to dissect the absurd journey they'd all taken. Remember the time he said he'd fix everything with a magic wand? someone chuckled, and a chorus of laughter filled the air, echoing the ridiculousness of those fantastical claims. But beneath the giggles, deeper reflections began surfacing with each retelling. Had they truly been bamboozled? The humor was both a shield and a weapon, deflecting the pangs of self-awareness that clawed at their collective consciousness.

As laughter turned into light-hearted mockery, more profound questions began to simmer. What now? they asked, some incredulously, others with a sense of newfound intelligence sparked by the absurdity they had endured. The mood shifted slightly from comedic relief to a poignant undercurrent of realization—an awakening of sorts. While the farce played out, another act lingered just beneath the surface, waiting to be performed in the hearts and minds of the citizens, beckoning them towards a critical examination of their past loyalty.

What Now? The Epilogue of Promises and Lies

The election results echoed through the air like a poorly-timed punchline, leaving citizens leaning in with anticipation reminiscent of a cliffhanger on a beloved sitcom. It was the culmination of a season filled with politically charged antics, and the audience of voters found themselves uncomfortably wedged between a world of laughter and the harsh reality of their choices. They filled town squares, spilling over coffee shops, sharing half-hearted jokes about the charismatic puppet they had so ardently followed, as if acknowledging the absurdity of their blind devotion would somehow lessen the sting of the outcome.

As the final votes were tallied, the bright lights of campaign stages dimmed, replaced by a palpable tension that filled the air like static before an impending storm. Faces turned serious, laughter faded, and whispers circulated regarding the state of the future—a humorously dark uncertainty that made cynics chuckle and optimists squirm. What now? The question loomed larger than the giant posters of Gerald Grindle, with smirking faces still plastered across the fading scenery of a campaign gone awry.

Even as the magical curtain of election night fell, the absurdity continued. Citizens gathered in their living rooms, clutching popcorn, reliving each ridiculous moment of rhetoric that had led them to this very moment. They exchanged wild theories like teens discussing plot twists in their favorite dramas, speculating not just on their new 'savior', but on the lessons that, somehow, seemed to slip through their fingers like grains of sand. Laughter erupted mixed with groans of disbelief as the realization washed over them—this was not the triumphant finale they had imagined. In hindsight, it was an act filled with slapstick comedy where they had forgotten their own lines.

After the dust settled, citizens meandered through the streets, sharing anecdotes of pride turned to pity. Each declared promise echoing in their minds like a catchy jingle from a long-forgotten commercial. They chuckled at the images on their phones: memes of Grindle enthusiastically wielding a magic wand—a symbol of whimsical solutions that had long lost their appeal. Oren, a retired teacher known for his dry wit, proclaimed, "This isn't an election; it's a bad improv night!" The crowd chuckled, nodding in agreement, yet deep down they pondered the irony of their self-deprecating humor concealing a deeper frustration.

As conversations shifted, they reflected on what lay ahead. Would they learn from this mind-bending mess, or would they wrap themselves in reassuring blankets of denial once more? A diner filled with regulars crafted hilariously exaggerated plans of their next political crusade, brainstorming slogans worthy of a headline in a trashy tabloid, as their laughter filled the air yet again. They shook their heads, contemplating how the lessons of the past echoed like a fuzzy memory. The tantalizing 'what now' hung heavily over their heads, propelling them towards their next comedy of errors.

In the weeks that followed, reflections turned into humorous speculation on the resilience of the human spirit when merged with the theatrical world of politics. Citizens debated the future in front of half-empty coffee cups, pondering both the lessons potentially forgotten and the laughs yet to be shared. Lines in the sand were drawn with the wit of hopeful comedians ready to tackle the absurdity. "Next time," someone ventured, "let's aim for sincerity instead of a script from the worst TV drama."

As they navigated the fallout together, voices grew bolder, a chorus of laughter and hope mingled with rising rebellion. Citizens playfully devised ridiculous plans for the next election cycle, sketching ideas that ranged from the ludicrous to the downright absurd. The question hung heavy in the air: would they ever escape the gravity of packaged promises and theatrical lies? The crowd laughed at the ridiculousness while slipping cautiously into anticipation; after all, in this game of political charades, who could resist the allure of the next act?

Acknowledgement

I extend my heartfelt appreciation to my husband for his unwavering support and selfless dedication throughout the creation of this book, [Book Tile]." His tireless efforts behind the scenes have been instrumental in shaping this material into a work that I hope will be both enriching and worthwhile for our readers. His encouragement, patience, and invaluable insights have truly made a difference, and I am deeply grateful for his partnership in this endeavor.

About The Author

Nena Buenaventura, a dedicated healthcare professional, has spent years making a tangible impact on the lives of countless individuals. Through her leadership roles in Rehabilitation and Out-Patient departments 1 & 2, where she served as head, Nena has empowered patients to overcome physical and emotional challenges, regain independence, and rediscover hope. Her tireless efforts have not only improved health outcomes but have also inspired a new standard of compassionate care, leaving a lasting legacy in the lives of those she has touched. Beyond her healthcare endeavors, Nena is a prolific author with a rich and diverse portfolio of publications.

Books List Authored by Nena Buenaventura

https://www.amazon.com/s?k=nena+buenaventura

1. **Gout-Free Body: A Gratifying Journey**; The author shares their experience of becoming dependent on medication and analgesics to manage gout, only to discover that a balanced diet and natural remedies can provide lasting relief.

2. **A Roadmap to Success – Unlocking Your Potential through Goal Setting**; both in eBook and paperback. This empowering self-help and development book serves as your guide to unlocking your full potential through the art of goal setting and achievement.

3. **Questions of Controversy**; both in eBook and paperback. An incisive introduction that sets the stage for a riveting exploration of age-old inquiries and theological conundrums, offering

readers a panoramic vista of the intellectual odyssey that lies ahead.

4. **The Whispers in the Woods**; both in eBook and paperback. Is a haunting tale filled with mystery and supernatural elements.

5. **Chinese Deep Covers in the Philippines**; both in eBook and paperback. Is a riveting espionage that takes readers on a thrilling journey filled with secrecy, betrayal, and redemption.

6. **Seraphina's Wings of Hope**; both in eBook and paperback. Is a timeless tale of courage, empowerment, and the enduring light that guides us through the darkness, inviting readers to embrace their own journey of self-discovery and transformation.

7. **The Day Earth Decides to Rehabilitate Itself**; both in eBook and paperback. Is a comprehensive guide to addressing the environmental challenges facing our planet and working towards its rehabilitation?

8. **Memory Techniques and Strategies**; in eBook format. This book explores various memory techniques and strategies that can enhance memory and overall cognitive function.

9. **Creating a Successful Side Business while Maintaining a Full-Time Job**; in eBook format. This book provides a comprehensive guide on how to successfully start and manage a side business while working full-time.

10. **The Root of Health: Discovering Nature's Medicine**; this eBook weaves together history, science, and personal journeys, revealing how plants have been essential healers for centuries.

11. **Sustainable Living Made Simple - A Guide to Zero Waste Minimalism**; This book is your roadmap to a fulfilling and sustainable lifestyle. Are you ready to embrace the joy of living with less and making a positive impact on the world?

12. **The Lost Letters of Girona** – is a captivating tale that unfolds in the ancient city of Girona, Spain. The story centers around a mysterious package containing a collection of sealed letters, each a window into the city's hidden past.

13. **The Prince of Darkness The Defender** – follows the tumultuous journey of Alexandru III, heir to the throne of Danubia, as he transforms from a young prince to a legendary, yet terrifying, figure.

14. **The Midnight Train - A Murder on Rails - Where Secrets Ride the Tracks**. A luxury train, a glittering cast of characters, and a sinister secret...

15. **The Abyss of Shadows – A Grizzly Horror Experience** – Through the eyes of brave investigators, you'll uncover the significance of cryptic symbols, the power of residual energy, and the connection between the asylum's dark past and its present-day manifestations.

16. **A Fistful of Embers** - As the characters navigate a town on edge, haunted by past grievances and new enemies, they uncover a trail of embers leading to a showdown in a ghostly town.

17. **Against All Odds – Is Survival Worth the Struggle**; isn't just a book about survival, it's a raw and intimate journey through the depths of human despair and the tenacious spirit that refuses to be extinguished.

18. **Tilly's Treasure Hunt - Discovering the Joy of Sharing**; This heartwarming story teaches children the importance of collaboration, friendship, and the true value of sharing, leaving them with a sense of wonder and the understanding that the greatest treasures are often found in unexpected places.

19. **Rising Above Challenges - Inspiring Journeys of Resilience**; Starting with an exploration of what resilience truly means, the book distinguishes it from grit and highlights its historical and cultural significance. Through carefully curated personal triumphs, readers will discover how ordinary individuals have overcome extraordinary challenges, from personal loss and illness to rebuilding after failure.

20. **The Power of Persistence: How Determination Can Change Your Life**; provides a comprehensive guide to unlocking the transformative power of persistence. It delves

into the multifaceted nature of persistence, exploring not just its definition and importance, but also the mindset, skills, and strategies needed to cultivate it.

21. **Beyond Your Limits - Breaking Through Barriers and Achieving Your Dreams**; This book is a comprehensive guide to achieving your full potential and living a life aligned with your goals and aspirations. It outlines a step-by-step process for personal growth and transformation, empowering you to overcome self-limiting beliefs, cultivate a positive mindset, and take meaningful action towards your dreams.

22. **Voices from the Abyss -** This novel, set against a backdrop of ancient legends and forgotten lore, follows the journey of a protagonist who must confront a malevolent force unleashed by a cursed talisman. From whispering shadows in haunted caverns to the secrets buried beneath a blood moon, the narrative unfolds through a series of eerie encounters, each revealing a piece of a larger, terrifying truth.

23. **Living with Disability: A Guide to Maintaining Independence and Quality of Life**; "Living with Disability: A Guide to Maintaining Independence and Quality of Life" provides practical advice and emotional support for elderly individuals with disabilities living alone and on limited income.

24. **Voices from the Abyss – Warning from the Depth;** follows a team of explorers who embark

on a daring underwater mission to uncover the secrets of a mysterious sunken city. Their journey takes them deep into the abyss, where ancient echoes and chilling warnings whisper of a hidden danger.

25. **The Forgotten Child;** the disappearance of young Emily sends her family on a harrowing journey that blurs the line between reality and the supernatural. Once filled with laughter, their home is now a place of sorrow and dread as Emily vanishes without a trace, leaving behind cryptic clues that only deepen the mystery.

26. **The Clockwork Heart;** tells the story of Dr. Elias Faulkner, a brilliant scientist who creates a mechanical heart to save lives. Funded by the powerful Roth, Elias's invention is threatened when Roth reveals his plans to use the technology for societal control. Betrayed, Elias teams up with allies, including Claire Mercer (known as the hacker "Phantom") and Detective Marcus Hale, to fight against Roth's oppressive regime.

27. **The Moonstone Labyrinth**; *The Moonstone Labyrinth* is a thrilling exploration of the dangers of ambition, the pursuit of knowledge, and the struggle to balance progress with humanity. It is a story about the human spirit, the costs of power, and the mysteries that some believe are better left undiscovered.

www.ingramcontent.com/pod-product-compliance
Lightning Source LLC
Chambersburg PA
CBHW051310250726
48656CB00004B/1572